Contents

Growing Out of Debt

Acknowledgements:

We gratefully acknowledge a contribution from Barclays Development Fund which has helped towards the cost of editing this publication.

Thanks are also due to Margaret Cornell for all her hard work in preparing the texts for publication.

Cover shows external public debt indicators of Madagascar, from World Bank *World Debt Tables*, 1988-89 Edition.

British Library Cataloguing in Publication Data

Growing out of debt.
   1. Developing countries. External debts
   I. Hewitt, Adrian   II. Wells, Bowen
   336.3'435'091724

ISBN 0-85003-121-4

Published for the All Party Parliamentary Group on Overseas Development by the Overseas Development Institute
Regent's College, Inner Circle, Regent's Park, London NW1 4NS.

Printed and typeset by the Russell Press Ltd., Nottingham.

1:
Introduction
Adrian Hewitt, Research Adviser to APGOOD and Bowen Wells MP, Joint Secretary of APGOOD and Chairman of its Debt Working Party

Many issues of global economic policy can be left for the markets to decide. Others require administrative intervention to advance matters. An enabling environment is desirable. The choice of the most judicious mix of market and state intervention will of course vary across countries and over time. Financial issues, however, such as how to keep up debt service payments would seem at first glance to be at the 'market' end of this spectrum, and indeed there now exists a flourishing secondary market in Third World debt (a table of recent offer prices is attached at the end of this chapter).

But when issues of debt service threaten more than the balance sheets of some middle-ranking banks and financial institutions; when they put into question the economic recovery of poor countries after a recession and the survival of democracy in many parts of Latin America, and leave rich country governments facing in different directions according to whether they are wearing their donor hat or their creditor mantle, it is obvious that political initiatives are necessary and that a political lead has to be given to the lower-level decisions of the markets and of national and international regulatory bodies.

Such was the case when it dawned upon the world in the summer of 1982 that Mexico would never be able to pay its international debt. Granted that the package which bought time on this particular issue was agreed with and implemented by the International Monetary Fund, it clearly had to have a political steer to get off the ground. Another example of *collective* political action can be cited from four years earlier, when creditor governments resolved within UNCTAD to relieve the aid-debt of the poorest and least developed countries. (Fine political initiatives were only slightly perverted on this occasion by administrative intervention: Judith Hart, Lady Hart of Lanark, assures us that the civil servants of the creditor nations banded together in their collective caution and insisted on renaming this debt relief initiative a more anodyne

'Retroactive Terms Adjustment' — the 'RTA' it has been ever since.)

Political initiatives to make the debt crisis more manageable by addressing payments imbalances and simultaneously attempting to restimulate effective demand throughout the world have occurred thick and fast since then. When this All Party Group first took a serious look at the problem, in preparing its report *Managing Third World Debt* (1987), the Baker Plan, named after the then US Treasury Secretary, was in vogue. This aimed to keep payments from the fifteen (later seventeen) major debtors (mainly in Latin America) to the creditor banks current by pledging a new, larger infusion of both public sector and bank credit. It was backed by strict stabilisation programmes of the Fund and adjustment programmes of the World Bank. Thus, the acceptance of economic policy reforms — usually of a highly sensitive political nature — here too became the *sine qua non* of debt relief and restored international credit flows. A few governments which balked at the conditions, instead limiting their debt service to an arbitrary share of their export earnings, did not prosper economically or resolve their debt problems, but nor did the Baker Plan achieve its objectives — partly through lack of resources, it is true. Moreover, at the time of the above APGOOD report, we felt that too little attention had been paid to the debt problems of the poorer countries, especially in Africa, whose debts were mainly owed, and whose debt service was mainly flowing back, to the governments and international financial institutions which were giving them aid, rather than to the banks. Our inquiry and the resulting report was thus instrumental in advancing British, European and international initiatives on this matter — the 'Lawson Plan' of 1987; new rules for Paris Club reschedulings; new European Community actions for the debt-distressed ACP countries using supplementary EDF funding; and also the Wass report to the UN Secretary-General which identified a $5 billion financing gap for the sub-Saharan African countries.[1]

We dared suggest at that time that some debts were better considered cancelled, written-off or 'forgiven', although that was hardly the political currency of the time. Even at the time of the December 1988 conference which APGOOD organised in the Grand Committee Room of the House of Commons, on which this volume draws,[2] proposals for the debt reductions were still being treated cautiously (see Williamson chapter), if only because of the perceived or alleged threats of 'moral hazard', 'contagion' or (perhaps worse!) the settling of private debts by public funding. Instead, the dominant upbeat theme, to which this volume also adheres, is that it is still possible for developing countries, and the world economy, to grow out of debt and that it is in our collective interest to facilitate this process.

Political initiatives are now accelerating the process. The Baker Plan was in March 1989 to all intents and purposes replaced by the Brady Plan. While still targeting the 'mega-debtors' — Mexico, Brazil, Venezuela, Philippines and so on: but also Nigeria and Côte d'Ivoire in Africa — whose sovereign borrowing is mainly from banks, the Brady Plan admits that some debts have already been lost and will have to be written off. The Brady Plan assumes about 20 per cent debt reduction, not just more protracted debt servicing arrangements, and it uses the far-from-perfect secondary market in debt. It is not yet clear, however, whether the Congress, the international financial institutions or other G-7 members will support this. In any case, the Brady initiative will not be the last. The Miyazawa Plan has been rapidly changed into the Sumita Plan and Japan has a new range of proposals on recycling. The World Bank, after assessing in a number of recent fairly controversial reports[3] the 'successes' and 'failures' of adjustment strategy, is making modifications to those strategies. The IMF through the SAF and ESAF has become an 'aid donor'. Partly due to the work of UNICEF (see the Jolly chapter), many international debt relief-cum-economic recovery strategies now have 'a human face' and a 'social dimension', though they have too to promote efficiency in resource allocation and use. Lastly, we are awaiting with interest the proposals of the Schmidt Commission on Financial Flows, chaired by the former Federal German Chancellor.

APGOOD operates largely on the principle that by putting more copious, more up-to-date, and more accurately researched information at the disposal of decision-takers, the political decision-taking process is enhanced. Backbenchers and peers are not often in a position to take initiatives themselves, least of all on the international scene, but this way of working does enable pressure to be brought to bear at the political level. Many issues of world development easily cross party lines. They just need more thought, more research and more attention by politicians: often a consensus is easily reached. We are resolved to continue to operate in this way. We would encourage initiatives which, for instance, worked towards facilitating external debt repayments in local currency; in converting counterpart funds into productive investments locally; in ensuring that never again do governments or international financial institutions — with a vocation to assist *development* — receive back more in debt service than they are prepared to relend on acceptable terms. But the main role of APGOOD is to create the political will so that such initiatives will be taken naturally. If the next two chapters in this volume appear to set the Chancellor of the Exchequer, the Rt Hon. Nigel Lawson MP, against the Shadow Chief Secretary to the Treasury, Gordon Brown MP, that is exceptional, but areas of consensus can be found there and more fully elsewhere throughout this volume. Many of the succeeding chapters are derived from papers given at the APGOOD conference, *Growing out of Debt*,[4] which was held in Westminster on 6 December 1988. The spirit of that occasion, and the modus operandi of APGOOD, is perhaps best reflected in the comment of Monsieur Claude Cheysson, then in his final month as European Commissioner for North-South Relations, having earlier been French Minister of External Affairs, and now heading for the European Parliament:

> I was most impressed when I received a letter of the All-Party Parliamentary Group inviting me to speak before such a distinguished audience, to speak in a language which is not mine, so to speak here as a Member of the Commission, which has been subject to so much criticism recently — and I happen to be "one of the reds" in the Commission as I belong to the French Socialist Party. But still I am here! and I can express my admiration for the present exercise: a public hearing on such a subject. I really wish every Parliament would do the same, would have the same sense of responsibility, in particular, the European Parliament.

Notes

1. *Financing Africa's Recovery*, United Nations, New York, 1988.
2. Senator Bill Bradley was not able to be present, but offered his paper to this volume.
3. Most notably *Africa's Adjustment and Growth in the 1980s*, World Bank/UNDP, Washington DC, March 1989.
4. Authors' positions, titles and affiliations are given as at the time of the conference.

LDC debt indicative prices on secondary markets
(% of face value)

	Offer A	Offer B	Offer C
Western Hemisphere			
Bolivia	13	11	
Brazil	46.5	35	
Chile	60	61	
Costa Rica	12.5	13.5	
Mexico	48.5	39	
Jamaica	50	42.5	
Nicaragua	3	4	
Peru	8	6	
Asia			
Philippines	54	47	
Africa			
Cameroon	85	na	na
Congo	30	na	na
Côte d'Ivoire	28	27	na
Liberia	20	na	na
Morocco	na	na	43
Nigeria — trade notes	27	24	20
Nigeria — loans	na	na	23
Senegal	na	52	na
Sudan	8	5	na
Zaire	24	24	20
Zambia	na	na	22

Source: A Citicorp, October 1988
B Salomon Bros. January 1989
C ANZ-McCaughan, April 1989

2:
International Debt: The Way Forward
Rt Hon. Nigel Lawson MP, Chancellor of the Exchequer

It is abundantly clear that the debt problem is going to be with us for a long time to come. Certainly, substantial progress has been made since it first erupted in 1982/ and the more apocalyptic prophecies made then have been comprehensively falsified. In particular, there is no longer a serious risk of a systemic breakdown of world banking. But we are still a long way from seeing any of the debtor countries being able to return to the bond markets, and meanwhile the burden of debt weighs heavily on their peoples. This has inevitably produced doubts about continuing with the existing case-by-case strategy. Some, on both sides, are weary of what seems to be an endless cycle of reschedulings and renegotiations. And others have always been temperamentally inclined to look for grand designs and global solutions.

I have to say, however, that I see no acceptable alternative to each debtor country negotiating with its creditors about the best way to manage its debts. That is what domestic borrowers do the world over. And while borrowings by sovereign states do raise some wider issues, the basic principles are just the same. Moreover, the debt problem did not arise from any single global development: it arose because individual countries sought to borrow from individual creditors — primarily from the commercial banks, but also to some extent from governments and the international financial institutions — and the creditors, by and large, lent the money willingly.

Indeed, the search for global solutions is not only mistaken, but counterproductive. It acts as a distraction from the tasks which do matter: managing the debt that remains; and helping the debtor countries to restructure their economies in a way that will improve their performance in the future.

Sub-Saharan Africa

For the poorest countries in sub-Saharan Africa, most of the money is owed to governments and other public sector sources, and so the problem is one for governments to sort out. That is why I launched my debt initiative in April 1987.

Its starting point was essentially a recognition of reality. With debt per head at about $250 and GNP per head typically less than $350, it was hardly surprising that these countries were for the most part unable to pay even the interest on their debts, let alone to repay the principal. With the interest thus being capitalised, the burden was growing exponentially, and the poorest countries simply did not have the resources or industrial base to pull their economies round. I therefore welcomed — and pledged full support for — the proposal by Michael Camdessus, the Managing Director of the IMF, to treble the size of the IMF's Structural Adjustment Facility, which provides cheap loans for poorer countries undertaking agreed economic adjustment policies. The UK provides the largest single contribution to the interest subsidy of this Enhanced SAF and five countries have already benefited from this new facility. The UK has also pledged full support for the World Bank's Special Programme of Assistance for Africa, launched in December 1987.

I am particularly pleased that action is now under way on all three parts of the initiative I launched. Agreement was reached fairly soon on my first two proposals: the writing off of old aid loans and more generous rescheduling terms. As a result more aid loans are now being written off; Germany announced a substantial package along these lines in September 1988 and Japan has also undertaken to act along these lines on a major scale. At the same time longer repayment periods with generous grace periods are now being allowed when other official loans are rescheduled, within the Paris Club. This process began as early as May 1987, and ten countries have so far benefited.

My third proposal was a more radical one: to reduce the burden of interest payments, and it understandably took longer to secure agreement. First in principle at the Toronto economic summit in the summer of 1988, and finally in detail at the World Bank/IMF meetings in Berlin in September, creditor countries reached agreement on an approach which offered a choice of three routes to the common aim of reducing the debt burden, each involving a degree of concession:

● First, creditor countries can reduce the interest rates charged on loans from export credit agencies, by 3.5 percentage points, (or by halving the rate in the rare cases where it is below 7 per cent). The loan will be rescheduled over 14 years, with an eight-year grace period. This is the route the UK, along with most other creditor countries, is adopting.

● Second, creditor countries can choose to write off altogether one-third of the debt service falling due in the period in question, and to reschedule the remainder of the debt over 14 years with an eight-year grace period, but at market rates of interest.

● Third, countries unable to accept either of these solutions can reschedule their loans, again at market rates, over 25 years, with a 14-year grace period.

Mali and Madagascar have already benefited from these terms in rescheduling their debts. A number of other countries will be coming up over the next few months, including some from the Commonwealth.

Taken together, these developments add up to a very considerable advance in tackling the debt problems of the poorest countries in the world. By breaking the vicious circle of an ever rising burden of debt, this new approach offers them some light at the end of an inevitably dark tunnel.

The middle-income debtors

The position of the middle-income debtors is different. Most of their debts are owed to the commercial banks, and their management is emphatically a matter between the banks and the countries concerned. The commercial banks lent the money not out of a sense of altruism, but because they believed it was in their commercial interest to do so. Now that this judgement has proved sadly mistaken, there can be no question of taxpayers bailing them out from the consequences of their decisions, and most of the banks accept this.

The unwillingness of the commercial banks to lend any additional funds to the middle-income debtor countries has inevitably meant that an increasing proportion of new money and interest capitalisation has in practice been provided by the international financial institutions and by official creditors bilaterally, rather than by the banks. As a result, the proportion of total debt of the fifteen largest debtors outstanding to official institutions has risen from about one-fifth in 1982 to one-third today. But the problem of the middle-income debtors essentially remains, and must continue to remain, with the commercial banks. At their meeting in September 1988, the Group of Seven major industrial nations 'reiterated their opposition to transferring risks from the private to the public sector'.

How the banks handle these debts is of course a matter for them. But one of the most encouraging developments of the past year has been the increasing use of a range of market-based methods of debt reduction. Following major steps in 1987 to strengthen their balance sheets, by raising new capital and increasing their debt provisions, there has been a considerable amount of debt conversion amounting to some $25 billion since 1983 through either securitisation, via debt-for-equity swaps, or straight buyback. To take examples, the Mexican debt-exchange scheme of 1988 has meant that Mexico's total debt converted now amounts to 15 per cent of its outstanding bank debt. In 1987, Bolivia bought back a substantial proportion of its bank debts. And in 1988, Chile bought back $300m of debt, taking the total amount converted to no less than 29 per cent of its outstanding bank debt.

The majority of conversions take the form of debt-for-equity swaps. For the debtors, the debt burden is reduced, and additional investment generated, while creditors gain a new equity investment, with the prospect of long-term capital appreciation, in place of a holding of debt whose servicing and repayment could become increasingly uncertain. So-called exit bonds provide a means for smaller banks to eliminate altogether their exposure to particular debtor countries, while at the same time reducing the debt burden of the countries concerned and facilitating concerted action among those banks that remain involved.

Debt conversion measures are much more likely to be open to countries that have a sound record of economic adjustment. It is no coincidence that Chile has converted a higher proportion of its outstanding debt into equity than any other middle-income country. Similarly, those countries with a good economic record have proved better able to avoid capital flight, and indeed to attract fresh capital from overseas. This underlines the cardinal importance of the debtor countries' pursuing the right policies. Without such a prerequisite for access to further finance, we would all be throwing good money after bad.

It is therefore vital that the IMF and the World Bank should continue to insist on adequate adjustment programmes. Inadequate programmes help nobody. They make it difficult, if not impossible, to attract support from the banks. They do not give those creditors who do come in a fair chance of a return on their money. And by delaying the return to genuine creditworthiness, and hence to the chance to benefit fully from the growth of world prosperity, they do not help the debtor country either.

Both institutions have an important role to play in helping countries to grow out of their debt problems. It is essential that they work closely together, without in any way compromising the key role of the Fund.

Private direct investment

The World Bank and its affiliates are also playing an increasing role in encouraging the growth of private direct investment, which brings not just finance, but also technical know-how and management experience. The track record of public sector investment in the debtor countries is not an inspiring one, and it is abundantly clear that the most productive investment is likely to be that carried out in the private sector.

I therefore support wholeheartedly the recommendation of the World Bank's Private Sector Development Review Group that the Bank should pay more attention, in its policy-based lending, to overcoming factors which deter private direct investment. A new Bank institution, the Multilateral Investment Guarantee Agency, is now providing advice on how countries can attract inward investment, coupled with guarantees to investors against non-commercial risks.

The signs are encouraging. Private direct investment in the 15 major debtor countries rose from £4.7bn in 1987 to some £8bn in 1988. Most of this is accounted for by new investment in Mexico and Brazil. But direct investment is rising elsewhere too. The UK is already showing the way. Thanks partly to the complete removal of exchange controls in 1979, our private direct investment in the developing countries has for some time now been running at a level greater than that of the rest of the European Community put together.

Nigeria

The problems and possibilities of adjustment and of raising new finance differ from country to country, which is of course the rationale of the so-called case-by-case approach. In this context, I have one specific announcement to make.

The Nigerian economy has been badly hit in recent years by the fall in oil prices and, with some $30bn of external debt to service, the Nigerians have faced a formidable task of adjustment. The Nigerian authorities have now reached agreement in principle with the Managing Director of the International Monetary Fund for a new stand-by arrangement, and they have also concluded negotiations with the World Bank for some substantial new loans. Provided the stand-by arrangement is ratified by the IMF board, and provided there are adequate contributions from other bilateral donors, the UK Government is prepared to contribute $100m in exceptional assistance to the overall financing package, which will be largely additional to the existing UK aid programme*. It will of course be imperative that Nigeria, like other countries trying to conquer their debt problems, should persevere with domestic policy reform. Without that, no amount of overseas assistance will be effective.

Trade

It is clear that sustainable economic development is a prerequisite for the debtor countries once again to play a normal part in the world economy. To enable them to do this, the industrialised countries as a whole have two responsibilities which go beyond action to tackle the specific debt problem.

First, there is the task of keeping the world economy itself moving steadily ahead on an even keel. The major industrial countries have now seen six years uninterrupted growth at an average rate of 3.5 per cent a year, the best performance for over 20 years. It is vital that we stick to the policies which have produced this expansion, and in particular that we keep inflation under control. Steady and sustainable expansion in the industrial countries means a higher demand for the exports of the debtor countries.

Second, the major countries must ensure that their markets are open to those exports. This is, of course, a particularly topical issue, in view of the GATT Uruguay round.

Although many developing countries still protect their trade heavily, the IMF has shown that, among them, liberalising changes now outnumber restrictive changes by nearly two to one. In contrast, in the industrialised world, protectionist moves, of one

---

*Disbursements were scheduled to begin in May 1989 (*Editor's note*)

kind or another, including voluntary restraint arrangements and unjustified anti-dumping duties, have been in the majority.

World Bank figures suggest that protection by industrialised countries costs the developing countries more than twice the amount of official development aid they receive. We all know how the difficulties faced by the developing countries lead to calls for ever-increasing intervention, including extra aid, from the governments of the major countries. It is ironic, to say the least, that very often the best thing those governments could do would be to get out of the way, by eliminating protection and allowing the developing countries the market access they need to increase their exports.

That is why it is important that the Uruguay round makes progress on all fronts. With regard to specific agreements, an area of particular importance to developing countries is tropical products. In other areas, the job is to agree on a framework for future negotiations. Above all, we must keep the multilateral GATT framework going. This is of vital importance to industrialised and developing countries alike.

To conclude, there can be no doubt that the world economy is in better shape, and an important range of new measures is now in place. Even so, the resolution of the debt problem will be neither quick, nor easy. But provided all sides play their parts — and I can assure you that the UK will continue to do so — cautious optimism is fully justified.

3:
Ending the Decade of Debt: Making the 1990s the Decade of Development

Gordon Brown MP, Acting Shadow Chancellor of the Exchequer

I wish to place on record the Labour Party's commitment to new measures that will reduce debt whilst assisting development, and will bring an end to the vicious circle whereby, despite the Baker, Lawson and other welcome initiatives, the loans that were to foster development in the 1960s and 1970s have become yet another means by which essential development has been forestalled in the 1980s.

When in the optimism of the 1960s the United Nations proclaimed the first development decade, few would have guessed that by the 1980s we would be witnessing a decade of debt rather than development. And few would have imagined that the very problems from which the development decade was attempting to escape would have returned in such a heightened form to haunt us today.

Having fallen 10 per cent in the first three years of the 1980s, the per capita income of the most indebted 15 nations has yet to recover, rising only one per cent in the last four years. GDP in these debtor nations is still six per cent below the level at the end of the 1970s.

Poverty and malnutrition are now so widespread that 900 million people can barely move because of hunger. This is a poverty that affects one in five of the world's population and still shows no signs of abating; a poverty that in a country like Zambia means that in only one decade the number of deaths from malnutrition has actually doubled; a poverty that has caused 1,000 young children to die every week in Brazil, alongside a reduction in child health care and basic sanitary services; and a poverty that means, according to UNICEF estimates, that 50 million infants will die unnecessarily between now and the turn of the century.

How can we break from the vicious circle in which loans that were incurred to foster development are now debts which definitely prevent it: debts that have risen from $500bn in 1979 to

$1,100bn in 1987 and $1,300bn in 1988? And with debt interest payments costing $100bn alone, more than twice as much as all the aid given in grants by governments and voluntary organisations combined. This is a level of debt interest payments which means that resources which should be transferred from north to south are now being transferred from south to north.

First there was a negligible transfer of resources from north to south, then a negative transfer with the result that a net transfer from north to south of $35bn in the early 1980s is now a net transfer from south to north of $29bn in 1987. In Latin America alone the net transfer from debtors to creditors is equivalent to about four per cent of their combined GNP.

For the major debtors as a whole, per capita income has fallen by 30 per cent and imports have declined by 40 per cent since 1980. And the tragedy in central and southern America is that the commercial bank loans to the dictatorships of the 1970s are now strangling the nascent democracies of the 1980s.

It is an unacceptable, unjustifiable and morally unsustainable position that the transfer of resources is not from north to south but from south to north. I know of no attempted justification for a situation that was never intended even by those who benefit from it, never desired by any agency, never justified in any economic theory, but never effectively challenged by any policy initiative however bold in the 1980s.

No academic, no economist, no government has ever advocated a flow of resources from the poor nations to the rich as a way of stimulating the progress of the poor. But no organisation, international or national, has effectively tackled what is happening. And now we have a transfer of resources to the extent that the World Bank in 1987 actually took in more cash from the indebted countries than it paid out.

If these problems could not be sorted out in the recent period of high growth, with none of the repercussions of the huge US debt problem, it is difficult to imagine them being sorted out without new measures in a period when growth slackens. And all the predictions are that world growth will slacken. The 1988 UNCTAD Trade and Development Report predicts a growth in world output of around three per cent and that expansion in world trade will slow to five per cent from just under six per cent. Indeed the best indicators we have suggest that world trade will slacken from more than six per cent in 1988 to just under five per cent in 1989 and to just 2.5 per cent in 1990.

If, according to UNCTAD, the indebted countries are unable to raise output faster than population growth, and since 1983 nine of the 15 most indebted nations have had negative growth in one year or more, and at least three have suffered falls in per capita income every year, then they are unlikely to do any better when the world growth rate starts slowing down.

The damage to the industrialising countries is one thing, the damage to all of us is another. Senator Bradley has estimated that for the four years 1981-5 US exports to Latin America alone fell by 40 per cent and the World Bank calculates that Latin American and Caribbean imports from all countries fell by 40 per cent. Africa which is facing stagnation has seen its import levels fall by one-fifth since 1981. And one estimate suggests that since 1982 2-3 million jobs have been lost in western Europe as a result of reduced European trade with the Third World.

I would like to make a few comments on what we might do about this situation. Clearly endless rescheduling of debt cannot solve the problems. As the World Bank has had to recognise, no country has significantly reduced its debt ratios. Default is a dangerous path; present defaults on past debts deny the debtor countries future credits. Outright debt forgiveness, as suggested by UNCTAD, is not going to happen, although most case-by-case schemes of debt reduction would be valuable.

Three measures might be undertaken. First, to carry forward what the Labour government started in 1978, and to convert bilateral loans into grants for the poorest countries. Second, to ensure that export credits are set at low interest rates. And third, to oblige the World Bank and the IMF to set aside funds that could be used with less stringent loan conditions.

But the problems we face will not be solved by these measures alone, nor indeed by growth or lower interest rates, which are not very likely in the present climate. More must be done. There must be a co-operative and explicitly political solution to the debt crisis — an approach that is now recommended by people as diverse in their political standpoints as James Robinson of American Express, Senator Bill Bradley in the US, Lord Lever and many others. The scope does exist for a bargain to be struck between debtors and creditors (both public and private) to achieve debt reduction which will enhance growth and trade.

The Baker Plan was welcomed when it was issued in 1985. Yet it is quite clear that for all its benefits the Baker Plan has not effectively provided a mechanism for the growth in investment in the south that is needed.

The major lesson of the debt crisis is that international financial flows need public sector guidance. When the Brandt Report was formulated it envisaged major public sector and multinational initiatives to ensure that transfer of resources did take place from north to south. Today without any grand project on the scale of Brandt the public sector is having to pick up the pieces anyway in the wake of the bank lending that recycled the OPEC surpluses of the 1970s. With little new private sector lending being undertaken, the share of public funds in total financial flows to developing countries has almost doubled since 1980. The developing world is now more dependent on public finance than ever before. Those who argue that the market alone cannot guarantee the continued financing have been proved right.

Some people have advocated an extension of public sector grants and loans as a strategy in itself. That of course is to be welcomed and is essential. But if it only means that public sector lending will replace private sector lending, then resources may still be moving from south to north and the debt problems will remain.

What we ought to consider in addition is something like a public sector guarantee for private sector lending. The central objective would be to restore transfers from north to south, and in ensuring that this objective was paramount, to create an incentive for indebted countries not to default, together with a real incentive for banks to write down at least some of their past loans as they are guaranteed repayment of new ones.

Such guarantees would not be unconditional. The commercial banks would be expected to write off a proportion of their old debts, and a development scheme supported by new lending would not only have to contribute to economic growth but also demonstrably serve the immediate interests of the poor. Simultaneously the Group of Seven, or a new international agency, would tackle the problem of debt, the negative transfers from south to north and the fragility of the banking system.

A number of proposals already exist for the creation of an institution, perhaps an affiliate of the World Bank, capitalised by the creditor governments, which can offer either funds or guarantees to facilitate debt reduction. Such schemes might involve the provision of fixed interest bonds against which commercial banks can exchange at a discount some of the developing country loans in their portfolios. As a result the burden of the debtor nations would be reduced, thereby stimulating development and trade, whilst the banks' balance sheets would also improve.

In addition, we must also strengthen the measures taken to alleviate the African debt problem. Africa was too poor to be creditworthy during the private bank lending boom and its debts are mostly to public sector agencies. In fact Africa needs $5bn a year merely to overcome its chronic debt crisis which has paralysed imports to sub-Saharan Africa, and which has led to income per head falling nearly three per cent a year during the 1980s.

The last Labour government anticipated many of these problems. As Minister for Overseas Development, Judith Hart converted official aid loans to the poorest countries into grants under what was called the Retroactive Terms Adjustment. As a result £1bn debt has been written off, a quarter of which was owed by African debtors.

We can take a little comfort from the fact that recent British and French plans for the poorest African debtors do include some debt forgiveness, reduced interest rates and long-term rescheduling. What we cannot take comfort from is the absolute decline in the level of British aid for sub-Saharan Africa. It has fallen 26 per cent since 1979, a cumulative loss to the region in real terms of £600m. Britain's total aid budget has fallen by 15 per cent since 1979 to an all-time low of just 0.28 per cent of GDP. It has also sharply declined as a proportion of public spending. We must reverse this decline and work to restore positive flows from north to south.

The Labour party's approach would also build on the Lawson Plan and extend debt relief to multilateral and not just bilateral aid debts. The Nordic countries have proposed the creation of a facility to re-finance a substantial proportion of these debts. The World Bank has responded to the idea and is creating a special fund to which donors can offer additional aid. The fund will pay for the amortisation of some outstanding loans, thus alleviating the burden of payment to the debtor. The British government should be prepared to contribute to the Nordic scheme.

The World Bank should also be prepared to convert its outstanding soft loans (offered by the International Development Association) into grants. These IDA credits now amount to $29bn and future replenishments of IDA should be in the form of grants not loans.

Such a package of additional measures of debt relief combined with increased aid would help to break Africa's downward spiral of poverty and debt. Our strategy is to meet the challenge of development. Dogma has made the 1980s the debt decade. We must ensure that the 1990s is the decade when we move out of debt and into development.

4:
Debt Reduction: Half a Solution
John Williamson, Senior Fellow, Institute for International Economics, Washington DC

During 1988 the major development on the debt front was intellectual acceptance and practical implementation of the concept of debt reduction. It is no longer true that the only way of helping a troubled debtor sanctioned by the official sector or accepted by the banks is additional lending. Many banks now participate in debt-equity swaps, some debtors have bought back a part of their debt on the secondary market for a fraction of its face value, and some debt has been swapped into alternative assets with a lower debt-servicing cost. These all provide methods by which the burden of the debt can be and is being reduced.

The advent of debt reduction is welcome, but it is unlikely by itself to suffice to resolve the debt problem, at least in the absence of a markedly more benign global environment. Let me spell out the limitations.

First, **debt-equity swaps**. This has so far been the principal mechanism employed, with $10bn or more already swapped in 1988. A debt-equity swap typically involves a bank selling debt on the secondary market to a foreign company, which in turn sells the debt to the central bank of the debtor country in return for local currency with which it makes an equity investment in the local economy. This changes the form of the foreign claim on the debtor's economy from debt to equity, which may have some attractions in terms of improved efficiency consequential on foreign management and also generates a time-stream of debt-service obligations that is more responsive to the state of the domestic economy. But it has only a modest effect in reducing the debtor's net international liabilities — an effect that is dependent on the central bank paying less than the full amount for the debt that it buys back (i.e., splitting the secondary market discount with the foreign investor). Thus $10bn of swaps may have made a debt of no more than $2bn or $3bn in foreign liabilities (some one per cent of the debt to the banks).

Moreover, in some countries, notably Brazil, the pace of debt-equity swaps was excessive in 1988. Unless the foreign investor buys a newly privatised asset (a phenomenon that was important in Chile), the central bank has to increase the monetary base in order to provide the necessary local currency. (In principle the government might issue local currency debt instead, but this is distinctly unattractive in countries where the real interest rate far exceeds the real interest cost of foreign debt.) Some observers believe that the magnitude of debt-equity swaps played a big role in driving Brazil to the verge of hyperinflation, which explains why the programme has now been dramatically scaled back. In the future I would expect debtors (supported by the IMF) to be more cautious and to seek to limit the volume of debt-equity swaps to a level that the economy can afford.

Second, **buy-backs**. In March 1988 Bolivia bought back almost half its bank debt (using money specially donated by friendly governments) at a price of 11 cents on the dollar. In September Chile got permission from its bank creditors to use a part of its windfall gains from the high copper price to buy back debt on the secondary market. A part of the academic literature argues that buy-backs are a mistake from the debtor country's standpoint because they involve the use of money that it could spend on its own development to eliminate debts that will not be paid in any event. I regard this analysis as nonsense: debts that are not being fully serviced are an obstacle to full participation in the world economy, a constant source of embarrassment, and a potential disincentive to adjustment. When they can be bought back cheaply because some banks are anxious to exit from the lending process at almost any cost, it is foolish not to exploit the opportunity.

The problem is that buy-backs require cash, and — almost by definition — troubled debtors are short of cash. Hence any solution to the debt crisis that relies on buy-backs to reduce outstanding debt is liable to take a very long time indeed. Buy-backs are likely to increase in importance relative to debt-equity swaps, because it is more attractive to the debtor to allow inward foreign investment over the foreign exchanges and then, when it seems desirable, to use the proceeds to buy back a part of its debt on the secondary market. This has two attractions: it allows the debtor to capture the whole of the discount rather than sharing it with the foreign investor, and it gives the debtor a continuing choice as to whether to amortise the debt or to increase imports (or reserves). Hence, as banks become accustomed to granting waivers to facilitate buy-backs and as the need to subsidise inward equity investment wanes, I expect to see debt-equity swaps largely replaced by buy-backs. But that will not change the conclusion that both these techniques together can only reduce the debt very slowly.

More rapid progress will require the use of **debt-debt swaps**. This is why many observers have called for the creation of some international debt agency that could buy up the debt at a discount, issue its own obligations (carrying its guarantee) in return, and pass on the saving to the debtor countries. In my view this proposal does not qualify as a 'practicable solution'. I suspect this would be true even if the new US administration were not implacably opposed to all such proposals (which it is): the problems of persuading all the banks to participate, of deciding which countries should be allowed to sell their debt and at what price, and of garnering the public funds to finance such an agency, would be formidable.

What may be practicable are more modest proposals for debt-debt swaps that do not envisage compulsory participation by all banks or the need for an international agency to fix the price at which debt will be swapped. The precedents here are the Mexico-Morgan deal, and the exit bonds issued by Argentina in 1987 and Brazil in 1988. Unfortunately none of these precedents are particularly encouraging: banks proved unwilling to swap on terms and/or a scale that would have achieved substantial debt reduction. The reason is straightforward: the *quid pro quo* the banks seek for substantial debt reduction is a more rapid and/or more secure exit from their sovereign risk, whereas what they were offered was largely continued country risk.

The security sought by the banks could be provided in three ways: by collateralisation, by subordination, or by guarantees. The disadvantage of collateralisation is that, like a buy-back, it requires the debtor to use its reserves. Indeed, reserves cannot be expected to buy more debt relief per dollar if used in collateralisation than in buy-backs (which implies that the Miyazawa Plan is unlikely to get very far). Subordination of existing debt to exit bonds looks attractive until one learns that the necessary waiver would require unanimity on the part of the banks, which certainly places it outside the category of practicable proposals. Hence I conclude that a major role for debt-debt swaps would require the provision of guarantees for exit bonds by some public sector agency; the World Bank seems the natural choice for this role.

Unfortunately this does not at the moment look a very practicable proposal either, because it runs foul of the Group of Seven's proscription on any transfer of risk from the private to the public sector. Nevertheless I still nurture hopes that the G-7 might concede the distinction between their quite proper resistance to an *unrequited* transfer of risk, and the highly constructive role that the public sector could play if it offered a risk transfer as a means of *buying* debt reduction from the banks. A major programme of public sector guarantees or exit bonds by debtor countries that have put their economic policies in order — and there are now half a dozen, notably Chile, Colombia and Mexico among the larger countries, and Bolivia, Costa Rica and Uruguay among the smaller ones — would enable debt reduction to provide at least half a solution to the debt problem.

The other half is going to need yet another reconstruction of the debt of those banks that choose not to exit. It will require them to recognise the regrettable truth that there is no end in sight to the debt problem if we continue to insist that it can end only with a return to voluntary access to capital markets. We need to lower our sights and seek instead a situation in which the burden on the debtors' cash flow is cut to a level they can live and grow with under a wide range of contingencies; which eases the perverse incentive effects that can be engendered by a debt overhang; and which avoids the need for repeated debt renegotiation. My own candidate for a definitive debt reconstruction to achieve these objectives involves agreeing a formula based on export receipts that would place a cap on debt-service payments, with automatic rollover of amortisation and capitalisation of interest in excess of that cap. (Perhaps other approaches would serve equally well.)

A definitive debt reconstruction for non-exiting banks, like World Bank guarantees for those that do wish to exit for a price, is an idea that is not immediately practicable. But its impracticability resides in the fact that there is not, at least as yet, a consensus favouring its adoption, rather than in the need to persuade the banks to abandon their self-interest or the G-7 governments to reverse the basic principles they have been proclaiming.

5:
The Debt Crisis: A Monetary Problem which Deserves a Monetarist Solution
*Tim Congdon, Economist, author of The Debt Trap**

The Chancellor has maintained that there is no single global development which can account for the debt crisis. On the contrary, I think that the debt problems of the 1980s have been caused by very high real interest rates and that these problems will not go away until real interest rates return to lower and historically more normal levels. To develop this argument. A borrower is regarded as creditworthy if the ratio of his debt to his income or some other measure of capacity to pay is stable. We should therefore ask what determines the behaviour of the ratio of debt to income over time, what determines the dynamics of debt. A debtor borrowing money obviously has interests accruing on that debt. If he makes no effort to repay the capital, the debt will rise by the addition of interest. If the rate of interest is higher than the growth rate of income, the debt will rise faster than income and therefore the debt-income ratio will rise. In those circumstances therefore, where there is no servicing of the debt in the sense of repayment of principal, the ratio of debt to income will rise when the rates of interest exceed the growth rate of income.

Indeed to keep the debt-income ratio stable in those circumstances the borrower must make an effort to repay the debt; what he must do in fact is to have an excess of income over non-interest expenditure. It follows therefore that the likely growth of debt depends on a relationship between interest rates and the growth rate of income; in economists' jargon when the interest rate exceeds the growth rate of income borrowers must have a primary surplus, that is, an excess of income over non-interest expenditure, to keep their debt-income ratio stable.

---

*Formerly Chief Economist of Shearson Lehman Hutton; winner of *The Guardian* Golden Guru Award for 1988 and now managing director of Gerrard and National Holdings.

This argument has complete general validity, it applies to every kind of borrower. In the 1970s we heard a lot about borrowing, but not very much about debt. This was because we had very low real interest rates, in all currencies and certainly in dollars; in fact real interest rates were often negative so that people who borrowed money on the whole did very well. Incomes were growing and there was a negative real interest rate. This actually is the present US situation. Until about 1980/1 the GNP growth rate was above the real interest rate, and until that point the debt-income ratio in the United States was stable, just jogging along. Suddenly it leapt up, and it was at that point that we started to hear about problems in the banking system. This was the contrast between the 1950s, the 1960s, the 1970s and the 1980s; debts and business failures started to explode, not just in the Third World but in the US itself.

In the Third World, we are dealing with sovereign debt. The debt export ratio is the key criterion here; if the interest rate on a debt is above the rate of increase in exports then there are problems.

In the 1970s the situation was one of moderate dollar interest rates and typically in the Third World of rising commodity prices and rising volumes of exports. The growth rate of exports was above the rate of interest on the debt and the debt export ratio was kept stable; the countries were still creditworthy even though they had trade deficits. They were importing capital goods and the trade deficits were helping towards investment, but the deficit ratio was stable because the relationship of interest rates to exports was so favourable.

In the early 1980s, the situation changed completely. With the leap in US interest rates in 1981, real interest rates became very high, and the growth rate of exports collapsed with the worldwide recession in 1981/2 and falling commodity prices. This was when the debt crisis began. In the new environment with interest rates above the growth rate of exports, the debt export ratio was kept stable only if the debtor countries achieved trade surpluses; and trade surpluses mean net transfers of resources to their creditors in the industrial world which then drain them of resources for their development. This is a vicious circle because less resources for development mean slower growth in the capacity to export and therefore slower growth of exports, and the whole situation deteriorates sharply.

In the farm belt of the US too they have had a terrible debt problem since 1981 because of the fall in the value of farmland; there too farmers do not have the capital to match their debt and they cannot service it because of reduced farm incomes.

It would be incredible if all around the world people suddenly became much more spendthrift and financially irresponsible, all in the space of just a few years. One wants a systemic explanation, a single global explanation of why this happens. My basic argument is that it is the rise in real interest rates which lies behind the debt problems of the 1980s. The key need is to get real interest rates down, and indeed without a drop in real interest rates one is only talking about cosmetic measures which fail to get to the root of the problem. In addition, any kind of reflation in industrial countries should be through monetary and not fiscal means, because fiscal means are more likely to raise real interest rates.

6:
Practicable Solutions
*H.E. Jorge Eduardo Navarrete, Mexican Ambassador to the UK**

My task now is to speak about 'practicable solutions' to the debt problem and it is not an easy one. Debtor countries as well as other actors on the debt scene have been looking for them over the last six years — at least. It is still debatable whether any solutions have been found and whether they have been implemented.

Bearing in mind the economic situation and the prospects of most debtor countries, as well as their social development needs, one is inclined to argue that no real solutions have been enforced. Looking, on the other hand, at the banks' financial accounts, it seems that it has been possible to avoid lasting damage. At any rate, the sense of urgency initially associated with the debt issue seems to have been largely lost — giving way to debt fatigue.

Nobody will deny that sound, sustained economic growth is the only long-term answer to the debt problem. This has been formally recognised, at least since the launching of the Baker Plan, in Seoul, in 1985. Adjustment with growth was its promise.

Sadly, this promise remained largely unfulfilled and in fact very little or no growth has been the common experience of most debtor countries — in Africa, in Latin America and elsewhere. 'Stagnation because of debt' is a more accurate description of experiences so far.

However, the need to 'grow out of debt' clearly remains an overriding one. This need has been expressed many times, by many voices. Let us hear three of them.

In November 1988 in Uruguay, seven Latin American presidents signed a joint declaration stressing that:

> External debt is now the major obstacle for the region's development, because of the massive net transfer of resources to the industrialised nations.

---

*Now Ambassador to the People's Republic of China.

> In transferring a sizeable proportion of their domestic savings, the Latin American countries have compressed their investment capacity and, as a consequence, their growth potentialities, leading to a significant deterioration in the living standards of their peoples.

In reporting to the 1988 session of the UN General Assembly, the Secretary-General underlined:

> The development process has come to a halt in most countries of Africa and Latin America. The social and political consequences of this situation are equally serious . . . A durable strategy must reverse the perverse net transfer of resources from developing countries to which the debt crisis has given rise and which deprives those countries of resources needed for investment.

On taking office, on 1 December 1988, the President of Mexico stated:

> In the present situation, the external debt impedes economic recovery. The country cannot grow, in a sustained way, if the present net transfer of resources abroad, equivalent to five per cent of the domestic product, continues. This situation cannot be accepted and cannot be sustained. I will avoid confrontation. But I categorically state that before the creditors' interests come the interests of the Mexican people. The priority will no longer be to pay the debt, but to restore growth.

These approaches stress the same two elements: resuming growth and, to achieve that aim, reversing the net outflow of resources resulting from debt-service transfers.

I suggest that these criteria provide an adequate rule of thumb to judge the practicability of solutions to the debt problem.

A particular debt management technique or, in other words, a particular item on the menu will be a practicable solution if it contributes to reducing the net transfer of resources abroad, thus allowing growth prospects in the debtor economy to be restored.

This 'test of practicability' seems to have been accepted by the Interim Committee of the IMF. According to the communiqué issued after its Berlin meeting, in September 1988, the Committee agreed that

> the menu approach should be broadened further, including voluntary market-based techniques which increase financial flows and which reduce the stock of debt, without transferring risk from private lenders to official creditors.

However, it should be noted that the notion of debt reduction did not appear in the statements of either the Group of Seven or the Group of Ten, issued in advance of the Interim Committee meeting.

Nevertheless voluntary, market-based debt reduction is the key element in any practicable approach to the debt issue, because it is the most direct and practical way to diminish the net transfer of resources associated with debt service. Debt reduction has been attempted in various different ways over the past five years — with varying degrees of success.

First, debt-equity swaps appeared. They proved very popular with foreign investors and with the financial institutions which acted as intermediaries in the process. They were far less popular with the debtor countries themselves. Most, if not all, of the benefit of the debt reduction implied in this kind of deal accrued to the investor, little or none to the debtor. In addition, there is the problem of the inflationary implications of large-scale debt-equity swaps. This was the reason why they were temporarily suspended in Mexico and their limitation — or even their halt — is currently being considered in Brazil, according to press reports. However, I feel that most debtor countries are prepared to use debt-equity swaps as a limited, *ad hoc* tool to launch certain projects or to develop particular areas, such as tourism in the case of Mexico.

It would help very much if foreign investors were prepared to complement swap operations with some fresh new investment. If every dollar swapped (which, after all, costs only 40/50 cents to the investor) were backed by a dollar in new investment, the deal would be far more attractive to the debtor.

Then the concept of 'exit bonds' emerged. This remains largely experimental, but it is a feature in several recent rescheduling and new money operations. It facilitates matters for a bank which is no longer interested in playing the game. Accepting a loss in currently held loans as a price for being counted out of further non-voluntary lending operations, is an option that some banks have been prepared to use. There is, of course, a clear ceiling for this particular instrument: the bigger banks are interested in continuing to play ball and exit bonds are no option for them.

Debt to bond conversion schemes have been a further modality for voluntary debt reduction. They were tried early in 1988 by Mexico. In this particular operation, a very attractive new instrument, yielding 1⅝ points above LIBOR, and with its principal collateralised by US Treasury zero-coupon bonds, was offered in exchange for discounted old debt.

The auction of the bonds, in February 1988, allowed the exchange of $3.6bn of old, restructured debt held by commercial banks, for $2.5bn value of new bonds. It should be noted that 139 banks, from 18 different countries, decided to participate in the auction. The bids of about 100 banks were accepted, averaging a discount of 30.6 per cent. In this way, a reduction of $1.1bn in the country's stock of debt was obtained, with a disbursement of $532m to acquire the collateral. The debt reduction should translate into a gross saving of interest payments of about $1.5bn over the 20-year maturity period of the new bonds. Unfortunately, this modest reduction has already been eroded by interest rate increases.

Despite its limited results, the Mexican bond scheme opened up a new avenue. Along the same route, additional improved options could be implemented. If further bonds are issued, the collateral could also cover interest payments, on a revolving formula. In addition, the possibility of exchange at par for bonds carrying a below-market interest rate could also be offered, along with the swap at a discount, for bonds yielding market rates.

If such a new approach is to be tried, there should be a reasonable expectation that it will produce a debt reduction commensurate with the cost of launching the scheme.

Buy-back operations constitute another method of debt reduction, which has been used rather successfully by some debtors, Chile among them. The most recent operation of this kind was reported on 10 November 1988 by the *Wall Street Journal*. Some details are relevant: in September, it was announced that up to $200m would be used to buy back Chilean debt. In response, offers from 129 banks were received, with a total face value of $882m. Bids of 57.5 cents to the dollar or less were accepted, resulting in a weighted average price of 56.3 cents to the dollar. In this way, $299m of the old debt were bought for $168.4m, a reduction of $130.6m at an average discount of 44.7 per cent.

It is clear that availability of resources to provide a guarantee for the bond issues or to buy back the debt is a major restriction for the generalised use of such schemes. It is also clear, from the examples quoted, that without some kind of financial backing from, perhaps, multilateral institutions, these are rather costly ways for the debtors to obtain the market discount on their debts.

But not only the debtors have been active in launching this kind of operation. The *Financial Times* of 21 November 1988 reported that a US bank, the Irving Trust, had circulated a list of loans, totalling about $500m, which it was prepared to sell at a discount. The report added that in late October there was a particularly heavy selling by Canadian banks, and concluded 'trading in these assets has grown — while no data exist estimates of turnover in 1988 run from $15bn to $25bn'. Certainly not a very thin market.

Options to enhance debt reduction policies are now being actively discussed. To quote one example, in mid-September 1988, a group of American bankers, chaired by a former head of the New York Federal Reserve Bank, formulated a series of recommendations, including voluntary debt-service reduction techniques, among them debt exchanges, debt-equity conversions and exit bonds, complemented by additional lending. According to a letter to the *Financial Times* they recognised that

> if debt-service reduction is carried out co-operatively and voluntarily, through negotiation and mutual agreement by the principal parties, it would have the desired effect not only of reducing outstanding claims against the country but of aiding economic recovery and bringing about 'creditworthiness'.

It has also been argued that, in the present circumstances, the reduction of debt-service obligations will only be brought about if the debtor country announces unilaterally that it is going to establish a scheme aimed at such an end, and then starts discussions and negotiations with its creditors. The scheme should, of course, be a reasonable one, backed by the right mix of domestic economic policies. It should be clearly seen as the best possible alternative, or, in the words of Professor Mike Faber, who formulated the idea of 'conciliatory debt reduction', as the 'second worst option', in the sense that any other alternative will be far costlier for all parties involved.

In addition, it is clear that the inescapable complement to concerted debt-reduction operations are new money flows. This is not an impossible marriage. The communiqué of the IMF Interim Committee quoted above puts them on an equal footing.

Both debt reduction and new financing are needed if a net negative transfer of resources of the order of 4-5 per cent of the debtor's GDP, on average, is to be dealt with effectively and if economic growth prospects are also to be effectively restored. It is often argued that (a) new financing will only worsen the debt problem, adding new obligations to the old, and (b) that the commercial lenders are not prepared, anyway, to continue throwing good new money after bad.

I would argue, on the one hand, that commercial lenders should continue to make funds available, in order to keep open the possibilities of 'growing out of debt' and, on the other hand, that the additional debt burden can be avoided if the external savings funnelled to developing countries are made up of the right mix of official, concessional lending, loans from multilateral institutions, direct foreign investment and bank lending.

Over-concentration on the last source, which is the most burdensome, produced the debt problem as it is known today. A balanced mix of the different sources should not produce the same kind of debt-servicing problems and should contribute to reversing the direction of the net flow of new external financial resources.

Achieving the objective of restoring growth implies both effective debt reduction and the availability of new external financial resources, on a continuous and predictable basis, in order to avoid uncertainty and to allow for adequate design and implementation of economic policies.

To ensure both, new initiatives are needed. On the debtors' side, in order to enhance the range of feasible options available, the debtors themselves should identify them jointly and provide a set of multilateral guidelines for individual debt negotiations. In this context, as the South Commission* stressed in a special statement adopted in March 1988, there is an urgent need for a debtors' forum, enabling the debtor countries

> to inform, consult and co-ordinate with each other on the
> debt management policies and procedures [and jointly
> explore] feasible debt management options . . . including the
> possibilities for concerted action for securing a just and
> equitable solution to the debt problem.

---

*The South Commission is an independent body, chaired by Julius K. Nyerere and comprising members from the developing countries acting in their individual capacities. It aims to make a fresh and objective analysis of the economic, social and political challenges confronting the Third World, and the ways to meet them. The Commission's inaugural meeting was held in Geneva on 2 October 1987; the Commission's *Statement on External Debt* was adopted in Kuala Lumpur on 3 March 1988. Mr Navarrete is one of the twenty-five members of the Commission.

(*Editor's note*)

The South Commission further stressed:

> Joint co-operative actions, involving both creditors and
> debtors, are the most desirable solution . . . [but, if this does
> not prove possible] the debtor countries will have no option
> but to act on their own to limit debt-service payments to an
> amount consistent with the requirements of their
> development.

Let me conclude by stressing a wider issue. Even with all feasible
improvements, the viability and effectiveness of debt management
policies cannot be taken for granted. Larger objectives should also
be addressed, which are related to the operation of the world
economy and to the functioning of an open and truly multilateral
trade system. Obviously there is a lot to be achieved in this respect:
— faster economic growth in the industrial economies;
— better and more effective co-ordination of macro-economic
  policies among industrial countries, including measures to
  eliminate or reduce imbalances and structural rigidities,
  particularly reduction of fiscal deficits to allow for lower interest
  rates, and structural adjustment programmes to facilitate the
  dismantling of protectionist barriers;
— adequate realignment and greater stability of exchange rates;
— resolute resistance of protectionist pressures and avoidance of
  restrictive trade measures;
— willingness to recognise and implement special, non-reciprocal
  treatment for developing country exports and,
— effective schemes for the stabilisation of commodity prices and
  more adequate compensatory financing facilities.
  Concerted action in all these interconnected areas is both urgent
and imperative, in order to enhance export opportunities and
restore prospects for sustained growth in the debtor countries. In
an increasingly interdependent world economy, a global, positive
response to the debt issue — and to the interrelated questions of
trade and financing — will be in the interest not only of the debtor
countries, but of the international community in its entirety.

7:
The African Problem
H.E. Dr J.L.S. Abbey, High Commissioner for Ghana

The unfavourable international environment during most of the 1980s, with relatively low growth in the industrialised countries, high real interest rates, protectionist barriers and a general deterioration in the developing countries' external terms of trade, combined at times with inappropriate domestic policies, has led to the emergence of the present debt crisis with no less than 20 of the poorest countries in sub-Saharan Africa (SSA) described as debt-distressed. On the basis of IMF data, it is estimated that the external debt of all capital-importing countries *nearly doubled* between 1980 and 1987 to about US$1.2 trillion. Over the same period Africa's external debt grew *at the same rate* to slightly over US$200bn (about 17 per cent of the whole), roughly half of it owed by the countries of SSA excluding South Africa. When considered in these terms, the debt problem of SSA is relatively insignificant nor could it be seen as threatening the stability of the international monetary system. Nearly 60 per cent of SSA debt is to public finance institutions — 10 per cent to bilateral Official Development Assistance institutions, and 30 per cent to Export Credit agencies; and 20 per cent to multilateral development finance institutions, particularly the World Bank group and the African Development Bank, with another seven per cent or so to the IMF.

However, the need to evolve a strategy of growing out of debt is perhaps more urgent in the African context, because Africa has been notable in the 1980s for its continued trend of falling rates of economic growth, already in evidence during the 1970s, and a more pronounced decline in the external terms of trade. While Africa's debt in absolute terms grew at the same rate over the period 1980-7 as that for the Third World as a whole, in terms of exports of goods and services, it grew considerably faster because of differences in export performance. Thus whereas the ratio of Third World debt to the value of export earnings rose from 114 to 172 per cent, for Africa, it increased from less than 100 per cent in

1980 to almost 250 per cent in 1987, and for SSA (excluding Nigeria and South Africa) to 325 per cent. The corresponding ratio of 500 per cent for the poorest countries of SSA — those eligible for IDA credits and the IMF's ESAF — is even more frightening; their stock of external debt at the end of 1987 was equivalent to five times total earnings from the export of goods and services and regrettably there are some countries with ratios well over 1,000 per cent.

It may be correctly argued that the debt-export earnings ratio is an inadequate measure of the burden of debt; among other things, it says nothing about the terms and maturity structure of the stock of debt. The debt-service ratio may be a less distorted measure. In 1980 Africa's debt-service ratio was 14 per cent as compared with 19 per cent for the Third World as a whole, due to its lower overall indebtedness as well as the softer average terms. By 1987, the debt-service ratio of the Third World had marginally increased to 20 per cent, but Africa's had nearly doubled to 25 per cent — and this despite large-scale reschedulings for an increasing number of countries. Without rescheduling, several African countries would have been required to make debt-service payments in excess of their total export earnings in 1987.

In March 1988, Mozambique informed its official creditors that it was having difficulty in meeting its obligations under the Paris Club agreement signed barely nine months before. As against total export receipts of US$85m for 1987, its debt-service obligations amounted to US$87m. The situation for 1988 was likely to be worse still with programmed debt-service payments standing at US$130m, against expected export earnings of US$100m. And yet Mozambique's rescheduling agreement with the Paris Club had been welcomed for its unprecedented concessionality.

There are some 22 SSA countries that the World Bank has classified as low-income 'debt-distressed' countries (LIDDs), which would be obliged to pay in excess of 30 per cent of their export earnings each year over the period 1988-90, if contractual payments were to be honoured. Over the period 1984-8 they in fact managed to pay an average 14 per cent of export receipts in debt service, and over the period 1975-86 were engaged in no less than 71 rescheduling agreements. In 1986 when Africa's export earnings fell sharply in absolute terms, the poorest of them managed to pay less than 40 per cent of the scheduled amounts due.

No hard and fast rule can be made as to the appropriate limit to the debt-service ratio. The resources that African countries need to reverse the decline of imports, for the rehabilitation of their social infrastructure and to invest in productive, and particularly export, activities need not all come from their own export earnings, though ultimately that is what growing out of debt implies. Discussions of the debt problem which have been unduly focused on debt relief have at times rather misleadingly created the impression that the possibilities for adequate growth can be inferred from the level of the debt-service ratio. Until the early 1970s both lenders and borrowers were generally careful to keep the debt-service ratio to a maximum of 20 per cent — an arbitrary rule of thumb, whose wisdom was widely acknowledged. The rationale recognised the need to keep enough foreign exchange resources, after meeting debt-service obligations, to finance those imports which could not conveniently be financed from aid and other tied loans. About 80 per cent of export earnings was thought to be the minimum needed for this purpose. As conditions change, any such rule of thumb may become inappropriate for assessing the burden of debt. Knowledge of import requirements to achieve a desirable economic growth rate (preferably in the context of a well designed structural adjustment programme), likely size of export earnings, the size, nature and quality of external inflows available to finance imports is needed before the debt-service ratio can be put into proper perspective. Needless to say, in a period of continuing deterioration in the external terms of trade, a zero debt-service ratio does not assure adequate imports to sustain growth and development.

In promoting a strategy of growing out of debt, more new money and debt relief will both be needed. Even on rather optimistic assumptions about export performance, the World Bank argues that US$2bn extra is needed by the LIDDs, and the Wass Report to the United Nations has estimated that about US$5bn per year will be needed for SSA as a whole. Though the focus and approach of these studies differ, the unmistakable fact remains that currently available external resources are plainly inadequate. The job of quantifying flows is notoriously dangerous and even the best of estimates must be used with the utmost caution. With this caveat the following set attributed to the United Nations is quite revealing. In the period 1979/81 to 1985/7 it is estimated that terms of trade deteriorations alone cost African economies nearly US$3bn annually; increased interest payments cost a further US$2.1bn; reduced flows of net credit and direct investment cost US$2.6bn;

all set against increased official grants of US$1.1bn. This adds up to a net annual deterioration in Africa's external position of some US$6.5bn.

The progress with debt relief has also been disappointing. From the beginning of debt reschedulings in 1956 to the end of 1987, SSA countries had rescheduled over US$20bn in repayments falling due, the bulk of them in the decade 1977-87. In 1984-7, over 60 per cent of all Paris Club rescheduling agreements were with SSA countries, several of which were involved in more than one rescheduling, one no less than nine times since the inception of the Paris Club and another six times in the 1980s.

One of the most distressing aspects of this rescheduling is the use of market-based interest rates. The conventional Paris Club treatment has dramatically increased the outstanding debt as well as its interest cost to African countries. A recent World Bank study instanced the case of one country where, over a seven-year period, capitalised interest resulting from Paris Club reschedulings added the equivalent of one-fifth to the stock of debt outstanding, roughly equal to the total of all new net long-term borrowing contracted during the same period. Furthermore, IMF projections for the same country show that unless there is a change of interest rate policy at the Paris Club, the debt-GDP ratio will continue to rise. The present practice of capitalising the difference between what creditors have agreed debtor countries could pay in the past and notional 'market-based rates' has resulted in an artificial inflation of outstanding debt to alarming proportions. Not only does this account for a significant percentage of some countries' nominal external debt, but the percentage grows with each new conventional rescheduling.

A market shift in donor and creditor attitudes to the LIDDs occurred in 1987. From April of that year, LIDDs have been given longer grace and repayment periods on rescheduling. In three cases (Mauritania, Uganda and Zaire) maturity periods of around 15.5 years with grace periods of six to seven years were agreed; Senegal was given a maturity period of 16.5 years with a seven-year grace period; while Guinea-Bissau, Mozambique and Somalia rescheduled with 20-21 years maturity periods and grace periods of up to 11.5 years. Viewed against the background of conventional reschedulings with maturity periods of 10 years including five-year grace periods, however, it is clear that the extra benefits in the extension of the grace period only accrue in the medium term.

There are strong moral, political and economic reasons to support a growing-out-of-debt strategy for Africa. Above all, the strategy calls for growth-oriented structural adjustment programmes, indeed with *growth per capita of population* as a major objective. More than 20 African countries now have adjustment programmes sanctioned by the international financial institutions, but several critics still find them insufficiently growth-oriented. They argue that programmes supported by the IMF might even be detrimental to economic development. In response to such criticism, Alassane Ouattara, the Director of the IMF's African Department, has insisted that 'economic activity in countries implementing Fund-supported adjustment programs has, in most cases, been maintained at a higher level than would have been possible otherwise', that such 'programs have typically improved efficiency in the use of existing resources' and in addition that 'the Fund provided direct financial support of these programs and helped catalyze considerable amounts of assistance from other creditors . . . In the absence of this support, the levels of imports, investment, output, and employment in these countries would unquestionably have been much lower'.

The fact remains, however, that conventional Fund-supported programmes of adjustment cannot be an adequate basis for a growing-out-of-debt strategy. It has been noted that 'even after rescheduling all eligible repayments and running up arrears besides, some countries are now faced with the fact that contractual repayments to the multilateral institutions are beyond their reasonable means'. As a result some five SSA countries have been declared ineligible to use Fund resources. Of perhaps greater significance for the on-going efforts to fashion an implementable, internationally supported growing-out-of-debt strategy, is the realisation in the Fund itself of the inadequacies of its conventional short-term approach. Again to quote Ouattara: 'Recent experience has demonstrated that political and social pressures make it difficult to persevere with adjustment policies in the context of a stagnant or shrinking economy. Sustained progress toward a viable external position can only be achieved against the background of economic growth at an *adequate pace*' (emphasis added).

It is to the credit of the international community that much has changed in the 1980s. In addition to the innovations at the Paris Club especially since 1987, progress has been made in the implementation of the Lawson Proposals. The commitments made by the Group of Seven at the Toronto Summit of 1988 will no doubt provide further debt relief. Following a 'thorough review of the main features of Fund-supported programs and of the facilities of the Fund' several modifications have been made at the IMF, 'the most important for the low-income countries being the establishment of the Structural Adjustment Facility (SAF) and the Enhanced Structural Adjustment Facility (ESAF), with the express purpose of assisting low-income countries with protracted balance of payments problems in their efforts to remove structural impediments to growth', through programmes designed over a three-year period with long-term, lower cost financing. Another important adaptation of the Fund's facilities is the 'modification of the compensatory financing facility (CFF) to incorporate into Fund programs an external contingency mechanism (ECM)'. The resulting Compensatory and Contingency Financing Facility (CCFF) is to provide greater protection of adjustment programmes from external shocks. The World Bank has launched a Special Programme of Assistance to increase aid flows to the LIDDs in support of economic reform, and has committed itself to allocating at least half of the US$12.4bn IDA-8 replenishment to Africa. It has also organised an increasing number of Consultative Groups for African countries. Positive developments have also taken place at the African Development Fund and the African Development Bank. An expected redirection of reflows to the European Development Fund into new lending will give a further growth-orientation to adjustment programmes.

These laudable achievements bear witness to the increasing recognition by the international community that African countries cannot turn the corner on their own, even with strong adjustment efforts. The commodity markets of critical importance to them remain depressed, however, and medium-term projections of their external terms of trade are generally adverse. Above all, significant gaps remain in development finance requirements. Aid targets solemnly accepted (in percentage of GNP to reflect donor capacity) have been so completely set aside that bilateral donors almost without exception measure their achievements in terms of increases in absolute disbursements often uncorrected for inflation. Africa needs a growing-out-of-debt strategy. It is also clear that the current international environment is still not adequately supportive of such a strategy. It must be the hope of Africa that the United Kingdom can show the will and the way forward.

8:
Six Principles for a Revitalised Debt Strategy
Moeen A. Qureshi, Senior Vice-President, Operations, World Bank

The crisis of the highly indebted middle-income developing countries is now entering a new and increasingly demanding phase. Not only to weather it, but to emerge from it on the road back to economic health, the debtor states, the commercial banks and the creditor governments must work together more closely than ever and must set themselves some revised guidelines for action.

Before I put forward my own six principles for the next stage of an international debt work-out strategy, let me set the scene in a few relatively quick strokes, and also explain why I set aside the debt problems of the low-income countries of sub-Saharan Africa. Their situation is critical but, as they are largely indebted to official creditors, the policy issues they present are somewhat simpler. Moreover, the recent Paris Club agreement on a debt relief menu has put in place the principles that can guide further financial support to sound adjustment programmes. Logic dictates that the proposed debt relief be extended to all low-income countries which meet the criteria and that this approach not be confined to sub-Saharan Africa. Otherwise this will be one more instance of an imaginative political initiative that has been prevented from achieving its full potential. For that initiative, Chancellor Lawson deserves much credit, just as the UK government and people deserve genuine thanks for their steady, generous support of the International Development Association and for their official and non-governmental work on behalf of the poorest of the poor.

Climate of uncertainty

The major middle-income debtors of the developing world face their own set of increasingly daunting challenges. On the one hand, they confront the challenge of advancing major economic reforms and restoring growth without falling victim either to inflation or recession. At the same time, they must meet current heavy debt payment obligations and attract large amounts of new outside financing. Either burden would be formidable in itself. Together, they can be crippling, especially because external financing — a key ingredient for successful reform and sustained growth — is at best uncertain and too often absent. Above all, these debtor nations require the assurance that external capital will flow in on a predictable and sustained basis to underwrite their adjustment and growth programmes. That assurance is missing. In its place is uncertainty and psychological and political strain, compounding the difficulty of designing and implementing sound economic policies. The severity of the problem facing these countries can be seen in the shift in net external resources available to them, from roughly one per cent of their GDP before 1982 to minus three per cent today.

In 1987, a World Bank staff review showed that most of the middle-income debtors *could* — I stress the conditional — grow out of their problems. That forecast was premised on their making progress in structural adjustment, on the industrial countries' ability to achieve stable, non-inflationary growth, and on the adequacy of external financing. Projections continue to confirm that such an outcome is possible. But the experiences in 1988 on a number of fronts — the behaviour of interest rates and commodity prices, the availability of financing and the economic performance of a number of countries — must now make our judgements more cautious.

In particular, uncertainty about external financing is putting the skids under reform. And as the pace of policy change falters, the inducements to attract fresh outside capital and credit diminish. The two forces thus feed on each other. If not arrested, this could eventually lead to an impasse in the debt work-out process.

Adjustment must lead upward

I believe this peril can be avoided. To do so, however, the debtors' domestic stabilisation and adjustment programmes — many of them commendably ambitious — must begin to generate higher levels of investment, income and growth: recovery, in short.

In too many cases, the very real progress in cutting fiscal deficits, introducing new taxes, removing trade barriers, promoting exports, streamlining the public sector, privatising state enterprises, reforming financial sectors and interest rates, and reducing real income in non-competitive sectors has brought sacrifice but not reward. For the 17 middle-income debtors as a whole, for example, real GNP growth rates have fallen from nearly six per cent per annum in 1977-81 to about two per cent per annum in 1987-8, and per capita income has dropped in many of them. Inflation has risen dramatically over those years, while annual per capita investment dropped by one-third from $400 to $270. In the Philippines, the 1986 GNP growth rate was just 40 per cent of the 1980 level, and while the share of the public sector deficit in 1986 had been reduced to less than the 1981 figure, investment as a percentage of GNP was less than half what it had been in 1981. In Mexico, per capita consumption is now 15 per cent below the 1981 level, and investment has fallen from 29 per cent of GDP to 16 per cent.

In other cases, policy advances on one front have not been matched across the board. Reforms will not yield the best results unless they are comprehensive, consistent and sustained over time. And some reforms — higher interest rates, for example — can tend at first to choke what is most needed: productive investment from both domestic and foreign sources.

The discipline required is of a very high order indeed. It would call for extraordinary effort in the strongest of societies. And such a level of comprehensive action is even harder to generate and maintain in more fragile ones.

Shortfalls in external financing

Essential as structural adjustment is to the debt strategy set in place in 1985, external financing is equally crucial. Uncertainty about its availability and adequacy is now undermining adjustment in three ways.

First, the policy managers of the debtor countries are also the debt renegotiators. They are being over-stretched by frequent negotiations with commercial banks, with meagre results, in addition to negotiations with multilateral institutions and the Paris Club. They thus devote too little time and attention to managing their economies and implementing reform.

Second, the actual volume of financial support for adjustment programmes is too low. Current levels of lending condemn the highly indebted to protracted austerity, when growth is the prescription most likely to make financial stabilisation a success. World Bank estimates indicate that investment in the 17 middle-income debtor nations is currently too low by at least $30bn or

four per cent of their aggregate GDP. Yet the goal of growth — and
I will return to this point shortly — demands the restoration of
productive investment. That is the end toward which reform is
bent. It is also the ingredient without which reform can hardly
proceed.

The *third* force hampering adjustment, however, is the behaviour
of a class of outside investors — the commercial banks. They are
turning away from the developing world debtors whom they
backed in the 1970s, declaring — and I take them at their word —
that the days of large-scale, general balance-of-payments lending
are over.

Some may be tempted to doubt their resolve. I do not, for the
following reasons. The past six years have brought fundamental
changes in commercial bank attitudes, strategies and financial
positions. The international financial system is no longer in the
highly vulnerable position of 1982. As they built up loan loss
reserves, many banks sharply reduced exposures in relation to
capital. Debtor countries have adjusted, and the frightening
nightmare of complete and total default has faded. Thus, bankers
no longer have the same deep concern about the viability of the
financial system nor the strong common interest in providing
liquidity to the heavily indebted countries. Moreover, rising
international and domestic competition and the introduction of
more stringent capital adequacy rules worldwide mean that the
key to success — and in some cases survival — for commercial
banks lies in building their capital bases.

The shift from the 1970s to the 1980s in terms of commercial
bank strategies has been dramatic. The emphasis on asset growth
that characterised the international expansion of many banks in
the 1970s has been replaced by an emphasis on asset quality and
on higher asset yields. Capital is scarce and low-yielding or
unprofitable businesses are being shed. In the case of a number
of banks, this asset shrinkage process is part of an effort to meet
the new capital adequacy guidelines.

Competitive pressures on banks are also intense because of the
continuing deregulation and liberalisation of domestic financial
markets. Understandably, commercial bankers have sought to
contain the developing country debt issue, to distance their
individual institutions from its effects as much as possible and to
redirect capital and management attention as soon as possible to
the new competitive challenges. Equally important, most banks

have found that their ability to raise new shareholder equity in the markets is closely related to their exposure to developing countries. The shares of banks with heavy exposure are trading at severe discounts to book value, while in a number of important instances, the stock markets have rewarded those bank managements that have been able to reduce their Third World exposure.

The competitive and regulatory winds, in short, now blow *against* the present debt strategy. That strategy has always been in the hands of the creditor governments. Signals from the governments, however, are at best ambiguous today and are tending to reinforce the basic 'every man for himself' attitude that is emerging among commercial lenders.

Governments or their regulatory agencies are pressing banks to increase capital to provision, to reduce their exposure to developing borrowers, to develop effective exit vehicles for institutions with fewer funds at risk and, at the same time, to continue to participate in the concerted debt strategy. Bankers realise that a shrinkage of the base for new lending will at some point undermine the concerted new money process or at best leave it in the hands of fewer and fewer institutions. Given the competitive costs of being one of those institutions, most banks have resolved to deal quietly with their own individual self-interest as best they can. For many this means withdrawing from the debt work-out process.

Countering uncertainty

To counter what could become a downward spiral in the debt strategy, European and other creditor governments must exercise strong leadership. For their part, major commercial banks must urgently display creativity and long-range vision. I know that both governments and banks are giving thought to ways of adapting and strengthening the debt strategy. From my vantage point, there are six main principles that must now shape thinking about the debt strategy.

Priority for investment. First, emphasis must now be given to increasing the level of investment in the debtor countries. In 1982, priority rightly went to debt-service relief through rescheduling and new money agreements coupled with IMF-supported stabilisation programmes. The second phase in the debt strategy was the 1985 Baker initiative to focus on growth-oriented structural adjustment. *Today, we need to move to a third phase: restoring productive investment as the key element in the debt strategy.*

I believe that the first two phases of the debt strategy have provided the essential foundation for a restoration of growth in the debtor countries. The Baker Plan, in particular, strengthened the debt strategy at a crucial turning point and shifted attention to the need for countries to adjust the structure of their economies to new realities. As a direct result of the Baker initiative, many countries have embraced fundamental policy reforms aimed at increased efficiency, trade promotion and better domestic resource mobilisation. The stage is now set for a new phase in the debt strategy focused on a restoration of productive investment.

Higher investment is crucial; without it, higher growth cannot resume. Moreover, more productive investment is needed to reap the benefits of the stabilisation and structural changes that are being or have been put in place by the debtor countries. And a larger share of this new investment must take the form of foreign direct investment targeted on reinforcing the opportunities that trade and fiscal policy reforms create.

Medium-term framework. Second, the debt strategy must now be cast in an explicit medium-term framework. The need for medium-term structural adjustment programmes has been recognised for several years now. Sadly, most financing programmes have not followed suit.

In the World Bank we put heavy emphasis on the importance of sustainable adjustment efforts, not simply year-to-year programmes. We thus draw up country assistance strategies and financing plans on a rolling three-to-five-year basis. The reason is simple. Development does not happen overnight. And genuine progress in economic reform must be supported over a multi-year period if the desired results are to be achieved.

I do not believe that the debt strategy can be sustained unless we find ways to marshal the support of all creditor groups on a medium-term basis. I am under no illusions about the difficulty that such a proposal faces. If anything, there has been a distinct shortening of the time horizons of creditors over the past two to three years. But this myopia is now part of the problem. And it must be corrected.

Role of official lenders. Third, official lenders will have to shoulder a larger share of the burden of providing new investment capital to developing countries in the future. Even for countries able to return to the markets within the next few years, the easy lending conditions of the 1970s are a thing of the past. Commercial banks, which came to account for two-thirds of the external debt of the middle-income countries, will not again be expansive financiers of development.

Discrimination and creditworthiness. Fourth, we must find a way to deal with the so-called 'tiering' that has taken place among countries, which is also reflected in the secondary market prices of developing country debt. For the reasons given above, banks are committed to narrowing the scope of their lending to developing countries.

The number of banks continuing to participate in new money packages is likely to continue to diminish. More importantly, the number of countries able to raise adequate funds in the private capital markets is likely to continue to shrink, at least in the near term. This contraction affects the smaller middle-income countries the most — countries where exposures in relation to capital are small and where there are no strong commercial interests to sustain commercial bank involvement on a broad scale. Indeed, for many of them, even the concerted new money process is in danger of breaking down as a means of mobilising needed financial support from commercial lenders. At the same time, there are a number of countries with good prospects of a return to the market. The incentives and the rewards for them to do so must be maintained and strengthened.

A case-by-case approach has been one of the fundamental points of the debt strategy thus far. But this discrimination among countries must be taken a step further to reflect the fact that, for many of the middle-income countries, a return to voluntary lending is very far off indeed. If present trends continue, failure to develop new and more realistic approaches for these countries will condemn them to a deteriorating cycle of inadequate financing, slippage in adjustment efforts, eroding economic performance and mounting arrears.

We cannot continue to allow the debt overhang to frustrate a restoration of productive investment in the heavily indebted countries. Where concerted new money continues to make sense, we must ensure that its amount is adequate and its flow over the medium term is predictable. In cases where new money cannot be raised in adequate amounts, we must have the courage to find new approaches on a case-by-case basis. In particular, we must not allow the fear of precedent to paralyse our creativity or simply be used as an excuse by those least willing and able to adapt to a new phase in the debt strategy.

Debt reduction. Fifth, debt reduction will need to play a larger role in the next phase of the debt strategy, although within carefully designed and country-specific programmes.

For some middle-income countries, the emphasis must continue to be on sustaining the concerted new money process. Large-scale debt reduction is inconsistent with concerted new money; it erodes the base for new lending, whether it takes the form of debt-equity conversion, exit bonds, debt-for-debt swaps or cash buy-backs. For these countries, debt reduction must be seen as complementing, not replacing, concerted new money and other forms of investment capital.

In other cases, the time may have come to focus on *comprehensive case-by-case debt restructuring plans*. Such plans would, of course, only make sense in the context of effective, medium-term programmes designed to increase productive investment. But where such programmes exist, the inadequacy and uncertainty of external financing cannot be allowed to jeopardise them.

In this context, many proposals have been advanced for new debt facilities or institutions sponsored by creditor governments that would take over the claims now held by banks — at a loss — and provide comprehensive debt settlements. It is useful, in my view, to keep the debate going in this area. But I am sceptical about the willingness of governments to take on the role envisaged by many of the debt plans now being advanced, particularly those that involve enhanced credit standing for existing as opposed to new claims. I do not believe that we have yet exhausted either the ingenuity of the market place in dealing with the existing stock of debt, or the scope for further regulatory encouragement of voluntary debt-service reduction. I shall return to this point later.

Regulatory adjustments. Sixth, the search must continue for ways in which tax and accounting regulations can be used to accommodate a smooth resolution of the debt crisis. Large national differences in the regulatory, tax and accounting regimes have weakened the collaborative approach as far as the commercial banks are concerned. Yet the legal form of most loan agreements binds creditors together in their search for solutions. We thus currently run the risk that the inability of creditors to agree the form and substance of debt renegotiation will force countries needlessly into arrears and prolonged alienation from international capital markets. Consequently, much greater effort needs to be invested in harmonising regulatory, tax and accounting policies to provide appropriate incentives for constructive agreements between debtors and creditors.

There are many possible ways that loan agreements can be altered and many financial techniques that can be employed to avoid the slide into protracted arrears when new money is not forthcoming. Reduced rate loans, portfolio insurance and interest capitalisation have all been proposed as techniques that could be implemented in a constructive way to achieve collaborative solutions. Yet while these techniques are attractive to some groups of banks, others find them unacceptable partially, if not wholly, because of the tax, accounting and regulatory regime in which they operate. Creditor governments need to study ways to encourage the use of such techniques. In some cases, policy-makers may only need to provide clear guidance in some murky areas; in other cases, the alteration of long-standing policies may be necessary.

I recognise that many of these issues can become highly technical and complicated. But there is also an underlying political issue here that calls for strong official leadership. These six main principles — an emphasis on investment, explicit medium-term financing plans, an expanded role for official lenders in financing new investment, greater differentiation among countries, broadened efforts to reduce debt, and greater regulatory flexibility — are, I submit, the agenda for further development of the international debt strategy. Together they constitute a basis for significantly reducing the uncertainty that currently bedevils the debt work-out process and is sapping the commitment of both debtors and creditors to a sustained, collaborative approach.

World Bank role

As far as the World Bank is concerned, we shall continue to adapt our country assistance strategies to changing circumstances. Over the past several years, we have dramatically expanded the amount of quick disbursing loans in support of policy reform measures. This has been necessary and appropriate as part of a general effort by all creditors to support countries during a debt work-out phase. We shall continue to pursue this approach in countries where it is justified by the policy performance of the debtor country *and* the financing efforts made by other creditors.

Let me be clear on this point. The World Bank is prepared to accept a large share of the responsibility and burden of making the international debt strategy work. But we will not take over the responsibilities of other creditors. Unless ways can be found to mobilise an adequate level of resources from the private markets over the medium term, we shall inevitably be forced to find new ways of ensuring that our own lending clearly adds to the resources available for productive investment in the borrowing country and is not simply drained away in debt service.

It is for this reason that we have given considerable thought to how the Bank should respond when comprehensive debt restructuring is required. We recognise that we are likely to be called upon to provide a large share of the eventual new investment financing in such countries. And we are keen to husband our scarce resources for this purpose. However, we also recognise that the official institutions may indeed have a role to play in catalysing debt restructuring agreements and specific transactions that reduce current debt service. We have always said that we are prepared to use our lending and our credit enhancement powers to facilitate financing arrangements that are in the interests of both debtors and creditors, provided that our role is genuinely catalytic and does not shift risks from the private to the public sector. This continues to be our position today. As circumstances change rapidly, our own role and policies must also adapt. Nowhere is this more true than in the area of the possible need for comprehensive debt-restructuring agreements in some countries.

Conclusion

I should like to emphasise the essential linkage between trade policy and a successful resolution of the debt crisis. No debt strategy can succeed if the debtor countries are given insufficient access to the markets of the OECD countries. Policies in the developing countries are increasingly set in the direction of more outward-looking, open economies. They are seeking to realise the gains from expanded trade, which include, importantly, greater efficiency in the domestic economy and a greater capacity to absorb *and service* external capital. For the industrial countries now to restrict access would not only undermine the ability of the debtor countries to grow out of their debt problems; it could well turn back the policy stance of many countries to inward-looking, isolationist approaches to development. Were this to happen, the whole world economy would be poorer. It must be avoided by OECD trade policies that continue to promote a liberal international trading system.

Moreover, we must not neglect the interdependent nature of adjustment in the industrial countries with the challenges facing the heavily indebted developing countries. The debtor countries today are running very large trade surpluses. Such surpluses are abnormal for developing countries and can be expected to shrink as investment and growth pick up, thereby facilitating the adjustment in OECD trade imbalances between the United States and its major trading partners. How important this effect will be depends, of course, on the degree to which we are successful in reducing the net financial burden on the debtor economies through increased finance for investment or more comprehensive debt restructuring agreements.

9:
The Human Dimensions of International Debt
Richard Jolly, Deputy Executive Director, UNICEF

In 1986, former Tanzanian President Julius Nyerere asked the question: 'Must we starve our children to pay our debts?' That question has now been answered in practice and the answer has been 'yes'. During the period 1986-8, hundreds of thousands of children in the developing world have given their lives to pay their countries' debts, and many millions more are still paying the interest with their malnourished minds and bodies. In Brazil's impoverished north-east, for example, infant death rates increased by almost 25 per cent in the course of 1983 and 1984 as a result of economic recession (UNICEF, *State of the World's Children*, 1989).

It is for this reason that attention must be given not only to the financial and economic consequences of debt, but also to the *human* consequences. Consideration of the human dimension is generally not part of orthodox analyses, nor is it the everyday concern of those involved in analysing the consequences of or solutions to the debt problem. Yet it is precisely because these issues have been given inadequate attention that it is necessary to underline their importance, lest the human tragedies and setbacks of the 1980s be repeated in the 1990s.

Moreover, not only are the human issues of great humanitarian importance, but they are also of fundamental *economic* importance, especially if economic growth is to be restored. Many studies of the sources of economic growth, both in industrialised and developing countries, have shown that to achieve economic growth, human capital is of greater quantitative significance than physical capital.

The human setbacks caused by the economic difficulties in Latin America and Africa during the 1980s are being increasingly documented. There is growing evidence of budgetary cutbacks in education, health and other basic services. Evidence from 37 of the poorest countries shows that spending per head on health has fallen by over 50 per cent, and spending on education by over 25 per cent in the last 10 years. In almost half of the 103 developing countries for which data are available, the numbers of 6-11-year-olds enrolling in primary schools are declining. More seriously, weight-for-age levels as a critical measure of nutritional status have fallen in many countries. Poverty levels have risen, which is reflected in Africa by a decline in household expenditures of 20 per cent or more between 1980 and 1987. As a result of the slowing down or reversal of economic progress, UNICEF estimates that during the 1980s a cumulative total of *one million African children* have died. For developing countries as a whole, the deaths of at least 500,000 young children during 1988 can be attributed to this same cause.

Two points underline the significance of this evidence of human decline. First, the deterioration in the quality of life for many during this decade is in distinct contrast to the considerable human progress made during the 1960s and 1970s. It is not just a case of poverty persisting in developing countries: rather, the poor have become even poorer and more numerous, a trend which is beginning to erase the gains of the previous two decades. Second, the consequences of the human setbacks of the 1980s will reverberate well beyond this decade. The failure to find and apply adequate solutions to the debt problems of the 1980s will be visible well into the 21st century through the stunted bodies and deficient educations of the next generation. Furthermore, these long-term consequences will extend beyond the humanitarian sphere. As mentioned above, studies on the sources of economic growth have established the crucial significance of human investment for long-term economic progress — a conclusion supported by the experience of countries like Japan and Korea. Moreover, progress in slowing population growth is linked to advances in health and maternal education, an area where spending has been seriously reduced by many countries. The world will be poorer and its population somewhat larger because of the failure to address the human side of the debt crisis of the 1980s.

Factors behind the human setbacks

The intention is not to suggest that *all* the human difficulties outlined above are the direct consequence of the debt problem. Rather, they are the result of a complex interaction of economic decline, increasing debt, high interest rates, declining commodity prices, and an inadequate process of national and international adjustment. All these factors are part of the total picture, often working together to reinforce the impact. In addition, national policies have sometimes substantially mitigated the effect of economic weaknesses and pressures: at other times, they have reinforced them. It is neither possible nor necessary to make a simple breakdown of the causes of these human setbacks. It is, however, important to recognise that the consequences of these factors combined are serious and require urgent intervention.

Nor is the aim to imply that national adjustment policies have been unnecessary. In *Adjustment with a Human Face*, UNICEF clearly makes the point that some form of adjustment is inevitable. To repeat the view of the Managing Director of the IMF, the critical question is not whether to adjust but *how*. UNICEF's point, however, is that the adjustment process which has often been adopted and which at most gives only marginal attention to human concerns, has had less satisfactory results than if full attention had been given to human factors from the beginning.

Are the basic weaknesses the result of national or international factors? The answer is 'both'. Too often, however, the international community has blamed national governments for domestic economic decline, while many governments have blamed international events. A balanced analysis must recognise that *both* national and international factors are involved, again often reinforcing one another.

It is equally important to recognise that international support on a much larger scale than is at present forthcoming is required in order to produce adequate solutions. As recent World Bank studies on adjustment have made clear, a sufficient net inflow of foreign exchange is essential if adjustment is to succeed and growth is to be restored, and (it should be added) if the human needs of vulnerable groups are to be adequately protected. However, taking into account loans, aid, repayments of interest and capital, there is now a net transfer of at least $20bn a year from developing countries to industrialised countries. If the effective transfer of resources implied in the reduced prices paid by the industrialised nations for the developing world's raw materials is also taken into account, then the annual flow from poor to rich countries may be as much as $60bn. Another source, the World Bank's 1988 *World Debt Tables*, shows that, excluding aid, the net transfer from developing to developed countries in 1988 was an estimated $43bn.

For African countries, it can be argued that their foreign-exchange requirements have been systematically underestimated, making it almost impossible at present levels to achieve a positive growth of per capita income over the next 15 years. A major increase in the net flow of resources *to* developing countries (particularly in Africa) is essential if there is to be a sustained and widespread resumption of reasonable rates of growth.

The need to rethink the solution

A number of approaches are required to arrive at an adequate solution. Common to all is the need for more attention to the human dimension. UNICEF has argued for 'Adjustment With a Human Face' — the systematic inclusion of concern for people in the objectives, content and modalities of adjustment processes.

Regarding the *objectives* of adjustment, adding a 'human face' means formally and explicitly recognising that protection of basic human needs must be one of the integral purposes of adjustment, and one of the basic measures of achievement. It must be emphasised that unless such objectives are clearly recognised and publicly stated at the highest level, those responsible for designing and implementing policy will not receive the necessary guidance nor have the motivation to incorporate such changes.

Regarding the *content* of adjustment, UNICEF's proposal identifies five main policy areas:

i) More expansionary fiscal and monetary macroeconomic policies aimed at sustaining levels of production, employment and general human needs satisfaction over the adjustment period.

ii) The use of meso and targeted policies to ensure that a fair share of the inputs for economic growth (i.e. foreign exchange, credit, land, water, skills, scarce materials, etc.) are channelled to the poor in an equitable way. Meso policies determine the impact of policies towards taxation, government expenditure, foreign exchange, and credit (among others) on the distribution of income and resources.

iii) A restructuring of production to give greater emphasis to generating income and productive employment for the poorer sections of the population — especially to benefit small-scale farmers and the landless, urban informal workers, and women. Any meaningful poverty alleviation strategy has to aim at increasing the incomes, employment and productivity of these groups if it is to succeed.

iv) A restructuring of government expenditure both between and within sectors and, in particular, away from high-cost areas and toward low-cost basic services for the poor. This would entail, for instance, restraining expenditures on high-cost urban hospitals while expanding expenditures on primary health care and such basic health needs as immunisation.

v) Special support programmes — often of limited duration — to protect the basic health and nutrition of the most vulnerable low-income groups during adjustment. Public works employment schemes and food subsidies are examples of such policies.

Finally, 'Adjustment With a Human Face' will require different *modalities*: lengthening the time horizon for adjustment to 5-10 years from the current term of 1-3 years; bringing a broader group of decision-makers into the making of adjustment policy, especially those with professional knowledge and expertise in the relevant social areas; and introducing a monitoring process that rapidly produces and analyses information on changes in the human situation and which includes data on nutritional status, health, and education, and not merely on financial and economic activities.

As innovative as human-focused approaches to adjustment may appear, the examples below show that they are not without precedent. If such approaches seem unusual, it is because of the current aberrations of modern economic analysis, not because a focus on the well-being of the vulnerable is strange in itself. As Keynes said of his own theory, the main struggle is to escape from habitual modes of thought and expression. Consider these examples:

— Domestic bankruptcy laws in industrialised countries recognise the need for creditors to leave debtors with sufficient resources to meet their own basic consumption needs and the basic needs of their businesses in order to generate sufficient profit to repay the creditor. It is not legally possible for the creditor to take everything.

— Under African tradition, it was custom among the Tuareg in the Sahel for conquering tribes to leave sufficient cattle to allow the conquered women and children to survive. How much more civilised than our international process is today!

— During the Second World War, the British Government was faced with the need to implement what were, in effect, two basic elements of an adjustment programme; to restructure production (from peacetime to wartime priorities), combined with the challenge of reducing dependence on imports. Significantly, the government combined this adjustment with the equally high priority of protecting the nutritional status of the British population. Programmes were focused on the nutritional needs of all age groups and were carried out with the support of Churchill himself, who in defence of this policy coined the phrase: 'There is no finer investment than putting milk in babies'.

In conclusion, five points deserve emphasis:

i) The *human dimensions* of adjustment and *long-term development* must be made a routine part of any analysis of and action taken to tackle the problem of debt. 'Adjustment With a Human Face' should increasingly give way to 'Development With a Human Face'.

ii) To achieve the above, *special measures* must be taken in which the World Bank and the IMF play the lead role, while at the same time obtaining support and assistance from other agencies, international donors and NGOs. Debt Relief for Child Survival is one such example.

iii) It is necessary to institutionalise the use of those *human and social indicators* that reflect progress in overcoming the debt problem. Such data should be collected, analysed and publicly released as rapidly as economic and financial indicators currently are.

iv) A strategy of 'growing out' of debt is needed — but this will only be possible if the international community provides additional support. 'Growing out' of debt will require that the current net *outflow* of resources from developing countries be reversed to a net *inflow*.

v) In order to mobilise political will and popular support for the measures required, the links between the human situation and the debt problem must be given more attention. The human dimensions of the crisis should not only be viewed in terms of the tragic consequences, but should also be seen as the basis for a solution through making ordinary people aware of the rationale for stronger political action. In this sense, the traditional anonymity so preferred by bankers needs to give way to development education and political mobilisation.

US National Security and the LDC Debt Crisis

Harry L. Freeman, Executive Vice-President,
American Express Company

'If trade crosses borders, armies won't . . .' This was the pronounced opinion of US Secretary of State Cordell Hull during the 1930s and 1940s.

An often overlooked US perspective on debt is a national security one, coloured by geography. Examination of the Western Hemisphere reminds Americans of a few basic facts of life:

● The only country between the United States and the USSR, as the crow flies, and as do missiles and airplanes, is Canada. It is not a purely trade motive that recently brought together two historically unlikely partners in a free trade agreement, the United States and Canada. As the leader of the US private sector coalition favouring the agreement with Canada, my most popular argument was that of US national security; we have a 4,000+ mile border with Canada, friendly and essentially unguarded, and we want to keep it that way. A free trade agreement increases the probabilities of continued friendship between its parties.

● To the south the US shares a friendly 2,000+ mile border with Mexico, the longest border in the world between a developed and a developing country. There has not been a military incident between the two countries since 1914. Mexico's population is now around 80 million, the US population is now 250 million; by the year 2000, the Mexican population is expected to exceed 100 million, the US, 275 million. This explains both the recent massive US loan to Mexico and the fact that President Bush's first unofficial 'official' meeting was with the new President of Mexico.

● To the south of both, but within intermediate missile range, lies Central America, a region of poverty and instability.

● More remote in miles, but sharing the same time zones and nonstop flights, lies South America, an area with heavy debt, heavy population, slow growth and recurrent political instability. At the moment, most of the South American republics are democracies.

● In contrast, Japan shares no border at all with a developing country, but acknowledges that the USSR is a large neighbour indeed.

● Continental Europe has a different kind of neighbour to the east, one that is less threatening in some respects than a neighbour which is both unstable and very poor. While Africa lies across the Mediterranean the poorest countries lie mostly south of the Sahara.

To the rational American observer, the Atlantic and Pacific oceans have shielded us from many foreign conflicts and problems for hundreds of years. This protection does not exist in the Third World debt crisis. The problem is literally next door. No wonder the US-Canada Free Trade Agreement. No wonder the talk of some kind of trade agreement with Mexico. No wonder the huge recent US Treasury loans to Mexico and Argentina. The *New York Times* of 29 November 1988 warned that 'in country after country, falling living standards are breeding a political decay'. With approaching elections and the rise of opposition parties which advocate debt forgiveness, the threat to democratic, market-oriented governments is real.

American rhetoric does not overlook George Marshall's tenet that 'real security must rest on economic prosperity'. I should hasten to add that I am not suggesting that this is purely an American challenge, but the US has the most to lose in the crisis.

It is with these principles and geographic perspectives in mind that I address the private sector's view of ldc debt, and, in particular, my own company's view, most often expressed by the Chairman, James D. Robinson III. We think the time has come for a more aggressive and comprehensive approach to the debt crisis. We think that the Baker Plan, while it has bought time and provided much progress, has run its course in terms of potential to solve the problem in an acceptable time frame.

Developing country debt — and I refer now to the debt of the so-called middle-income debtors largely in Latin America and the Philippines — has become an economic millstone around the necks of both the debtor countries and the creditor countries who trade with them. The time has come to resolve the problem and turn the world's energies to more intractable ones, such as the plight of the very poorest countries, the areas that still suffer from starvation, environmental problems, and other major world problems.

The case-by-case method, an expansion of the menu of the Baker Plan, might perhaps solve the crisis *over time*. Respectable economists can show us projections of how, over 5-10 years, with the 'right' policies and enough new lending, the debtor countries might grow out of the problem to acceptable debt levels, e.g. where normal, voluntary commercial lending is forthcoming. However, we are all familiar with present value principles. A ten-year solution to the crisis means less jobs and economic activity in all affected countries, increased risk of instability, and all the downside risks and aspects of lack of social and economic development. The opportunity cost, in terms of lost economic activity, of a delayed solution may, in dollar terms, be hundreds of times greater than the present dollar cost of the solution.

The arena is not short of ideas for more aggressive and comprehensive solutions. It is, however, short of the political concurrence and will to take the indicated steps. Japan can play a large role, and so must European countries. But the US which is the biggest economy involved as well as the largest lender to ldcs, must change its direction soon and develop a solution with both debtors and creditors. The creditor countries *must manage the problem*; if not, the *problem will manage them*.

To this end, my Chairman developed one specific solution. We even gave it a space age name, I2D2, which stands for the Institute for International Debt and Development. The detailed plan was meant to show that a detailed solution could be developed; some have embraced it, others have found it too complex, others say it is not politically realistic. The Reagan Administration took repeated shots at it with allegations of 'bailing out the banks' — an allegation with which we do not concur, namely that it would cost US taxpayers something they should not be asked to pay, as if they were not already paying something for the continuing crisis.

A core criterion for success is the linkage between debt relief and the reform of many debtor countries' economic growth policies. To achieve this linkage, we believe some kind of entity endowed with the power to negotiate deals, country-by-country, is necessary. We think that the most useful and appropriate locus for such a facility is within the World Bank and IMF, most probably two mirror facilities which can operate *de facto* as one entity. That entity, initially capitalised by the creditor countries, would have the authority to facilitate negotiations between debtor countries and banks to achieve debt relief, establish reform conditions in debtor countries, and monitor progress. Such a facility would exist alongside the existing menu offered by the Baker Plan. The problem is that for things to get better, economists tell us, there must be new lending and national policy reform. However, the banks have told us they will not lend more and the incentives for policy reform are decreasing as a result. Someone or something needs therefore to intervene.

Since the launch of our own proposal, we have been surprised at the support we have received from leaders of the world's financial industry, and that support continues to grow. We also note the changing positions of governments in favour of a more comprehensive solution. We suspect that a majority of the Group of Seven favour such a solution. We prefer that our own US government should join the majority rather than lose the leadership role in a situation where it has the most to gain and to lose.

Are we faced with an impasse? I believe not. What, then, will the change of administrations in Washington bring to this subject? The Congressional position has remained reasonably clear and consistent over the past few years. Indeed, the notorious, and much maligned (in Europe unfairly, I would say) Omnibus Trade Act of 1988 specifically addressed the ldc debt crisis. It provides both for Executive Branch reports on establishing an ldc debt facility in the IMF and World Bank as well as reports from US bank regulators with respect to the efforts they are making to help alleviate the crisis.

We do not know what the Bush Administration will do. We hear encouraging rumblings of reconsiderations, of possible policy changes, with the new Treasury Secretary, Nicholas Brady*. James Baker as Secretary of State has a new perspective which will weight the national security element more heavily.

Americans are basically optimistic, and the national security instincts of our new leaders, as well as the tenacity of our Congressional leaders, will dictate a new approach. As loyal friends of that Administration, but not above constructive criticism,

---

*The Brady Plan, which does involve debt reductions, was launched in spring 1989. It received a slightly premature airing in March 1989 when Mr Brady felt obliged to respond to the disorder in Venezuela. (*Editor's note*)

we shall be continuing to urge a more aggressive and comprehensive approach, and a rapid change in our official position for many reasons, not least for our own country's national security. The ldc debt crisis is much more than a banking issue. It exercises a broad negative effect on the world economy. It can be cured, and we urge that.

11:
Debt, Trade and the Dollar*
Senator Bill Bradley

The next US President will not be able to champion democracy in the world if his debt policies in Latin America impose austerity and demand from farmers and workers that they pay — in joblessness and hunger — for the mistakes of past regimes. He must master the conflict between debt and democracy or Latin American politics will master his foreign policy agenda.

Latin America is undergoing major political changes in which debt-induced recession could tip the balance. For example, there is a direct link between the 40 per cent drop in Mexican real wages since 1982 and the dramatic growth of political opposition to the PRI, and between US debt policies and the drop in Mexican real wages. The issue of debt was central to Mexico's recent Presidential campaign, and harsh criticism of the de la Madrid Government's co-operation with creditors produced the closest election in Mexican history.

Latin American democrats cannot stay in power if creditor demands make growth impossible. For example, the government which lost the election in Ecuador in 1988 took enormous political risks in 1986 to put its economy straight. Notwithstanding these significant reforms, Ecuador's creditors refused to budge. As a result, the debt rapidly became unpayable and an opposition that sees no reason to co-operate with creditors won the election.

With Costa Rica, the US Treasury's opposition to any form of debt relief forced the World Bank to abandon several debt approaches, including one to act merely as custodian of a guarantee fund and another in which banks were voluntarily to limit Costa Rican interest payments to a percent of GDP. Will Costa Rica's democracy become the next victim of creditor intransigence?

US debt policy not only fails to support Latin American reform, but actually obstructs it; the region's enormous debt is an obstacle

---

*Based on an address delivered in Washington on 19 September 1988.

to growth, but US policy aims to increase that debt. It has become the excuse for every setback to Latin American progress; budget deficits, inflation, currency mismanagement, credit controls, capital flight all get a free ride on US debt policy. As long as US debt policy remains so outrageously insensitive to political and human needs Latin America will not be obliged to face up to its own mismanagement or to pursue vigorous structural adjustment. US policy has become the scapegoat for any government elected on a promise of reform that suffers a failure of nerve.

The major premise of the Baker Plan was renewed large-scale bank lending: $20bn for 15 major Latin American countries. It was wrong. The period when commercial bank lending dominated development has ended; in retrospect, it was only a brief historical aberration. Real growth requires investment and investment requires resources. The Baker Plan failed to stop a net resource outflow. Over the last two years, the 15 Baker Plan countries paid $76bn in interest alone and transferred $43bn in net resources to richer creditors. The Baker Plan spurred capital flight by raising rather than lowering the level of debt and undermining the confidence of domestic investors.

Growth for the highly-indebted countries requires a true case-by-case approach based on the circumstances, effort, and policies of individual debtors. But the Baker Plan prescribed the same solution — new money — for countries as diverse as Brazil and Bolivia.

Growth requires reforms that can be politically painful. But the Baker Plan's bridging loans had to go out immediately in interest payments rather than being used to offset the political cost of adjustment. The Plan thus undercut the political base for reform.

Who benefited from the Baker Plan? *Not the debtors*; most of them needed to reduce rather than increase their debt burden. *Not US workers and farmers*; they lost over a million jobs as a result of the collapse in the foreign market that should have grown faster than any other. *Not German banks*; they had already realised their losses in Latin America. *Not Japanese banks*; Japan proposed a debt reduction scheme at an IMF meeting and a G-7 summit. *Not US regional banks*; they were prepared to treat Latin American countries like any other troubled borrower and give them some relief to restore growth.

Money centre banks bought some time with the Baker Plan. Between 1982 and 1987, they were able to count as income the money they lent to troubled Latin American borrowers who could not finance debt service on their own. By 1987 they also started to build their reserves even as they resisted interest and debt relief. But now even several money centre banks recognise that they can and must accept interest and debt relief as part of a Third World debt solution. Only the US Treasury remains a supporter of the Baker Plan.

A new partnership to solve the debt problem requires our developing neighbours to resist petty nationalism and open themselves to change, some of it painful. It requires the banks finally to absorb their losses. It requires US recognition that its own health in the 21st century depends on releasing Latin America's abundant talent and resources today.

In no country are the opportunities of partnership more evident or the danger of American neglect more ominous than in Mexico. In the four years since 1985, Mexico has met its obligations under any just concept of a partnership for growth. It is the US that has failed to respond. Mexico did its part in fiscal reform. It cut its operational budget deficit by eight per cent of GNP in five years. It also did its part in opening its markets. From 1985 to 1987, the coverage of its trade restrictions was cut from 75 to 25 per cent of imports, its average tariff rate was reduced from 29 to 14 per cent and its maximum tariff from 40 to 20 per cent. As a result, imports surged in 1988 by 47 per cent.

What have Mexico's creditors done in return? In 1986, they cobbled together a line of credit for $12bn — of which $9bn has been disbursed, none for new investment or replacement of worn-out capital, but all for debt service. True, Mexico got a slight interest rate reduction to 13/16ths of a point over LIBOR, but this concession was mostly cosmetic.

As a result, Mexico continued to pay its creditors more than it could afford. Money paid to banks is money not spent on US exports, or on domestic investment. Between 1985 and 1987, per capita consumption fell 8 per cent and US exports of wheat to Mexico plummeted 92 per cent. Per capita investment dropped 23 per cent over the same period; economic growth went into reverse. Per capita GDP has fallen 4 per cent per year since 1985. US failure to provide meaningful relief in exchange for these significant reforms makes a mockery of partnership and jeopardises Mexico's stability.

Reform and partnership are inextricably linked; that is the lesson of the 1980s. Without partnership there will be no sweeping reform, and without reform, no growth. Significant interest relief would permit Mexico to complete its budget and trade reforms while raising public investment above its dangerously low level. It would provide resources to cushion the impact of further economic reforms such as continued price decontrols, the elimination of domestic content requirements, and the repeal of anticompetitive laws. It would permit further relaxation of investment restrictions and create an opening for more competition in banking and other state-dominated industries. It would give Mexico the means to purchase more US exports.

What does partnership mean for the US? I believe the next Administration must have a clear view of what Mexico needs for growth. And those needs are daunting. Half of Mexico's population is under age 15. Its labour force will grow at the phenomenal rate of three per cent per year through the 1990s. Its big problem is jobs; but if paltry investment creates too few jobs, the country's unemployment rate will jump to over 30 per cent by the end of the century. A neighbour with 30 per cent unemployment would be an unstable neighbour. And an unstable neighbour will throw a wave of illegal immigrants across the US border in search of jobs to feed their families.

Mexico needs to invest enough to make output grow as fast as the labour force, otherwise wages will drop again. Gross investment has fallen below 18 per cent of GDP. At that rate, over two-thirds of investment simply covers depreciation, and the amount left for growth is just not enough to keep the economy growing at 3 per cent per year for a decade.

Where can Mexico get extra resources for investment? Waiting for new money from banks is unrealistic. Repatriating the money rich Mexicans have stuffed in foreign bank accounts would help, but that won't happen while the debt burden crushes confidence in Mexico's future. For the near future, Mexico will have to generate investment resources by cutting back the other demands on its capacity: consumption, government spending, and debt service. Given the 40 per cent wage drop, squeezing consumption invites even more political instability. Government spending cuts are out of the question; Mexico has already cut public investment in half and sliced overall government spending to 11 per cent of GDP, half the US level. The only other option is to arrest the outflow of resources to creditors in richer countries. In Mexico today, growth must wait until debt service declines.

Interest and debt relief combined with reform could very well be the only way that we can create an economic climate that would attract adequate capital to Mexico and to the developing world generally. Without an increased flow of capital from developed to developing world, human misery will increase, democracy could disappear, and our own economic future become endangered.

The new US Administration should arrive at its view on individual developing countries' growth needs in close consultation with the financial leaders of the other OECD countries. Drawing freely on IMF, World Bank, and Inter-American Development Bank resources, they should consult with Mexico on the financial implications of its reform programme.

The Administration must never delude banks into thinking American taxpayers might support a bail-out. But an involved federal government working with banks, creditor governments, and international financial institutions such as the World Bank could create a mix of incentives to restructure the debt and obtain lower interest rates for debtors. The goal would be to make sure the contemplated relief is consistent with the proposed reforms. Interest and debt relief is the *only* way to resolve the debt issue. Nobody wants to give our bankers unnecessary financial distress. But letting banks use bridging loans to make bad loans look good was a tempting approach that did not work. It is time for a new start. Otherwise, we risk financial and economic catastrophe. If we should fail, the new US President may well preside over a reversal of the new democratic wave in Latin America — a reversal more dramatic and tragic than the collapse of the 1970s promise of higher standards of living for all citizens.

12:
Global Solutions to a Global Problem: The Role of the European Community

Claude Cheysson, Commissioner for North-South Relations, European Commission and former French Minister for External Relations*

The situation in the Third World has been assessed and analysed in earlier papers. The Chancellor of the Exchequer took the same line as in his statement at the Berlin annual meeting of the World Bank and the IMF. I should, however, add a comment. Nigel Lawson refers to the satisfactory performance of the world economy, and he is not the only European Minister of Finance to stress that 'growth is picking up rather than slowing down' in spite of the 1987 stock-market crash. But I should like to point out that this is not true for all. Many people in our countries, and many more in the world will deplore that at the same time the poor became poorer and more numerous. In fact there has been a confirmation of a trend which has existed now for a few years. Things get better for those who contribute to growth; others are left on the margin, because they cannot contribute to growth, because they are poor, because they are heavily loaded with debt, because they are handicapped. Let us not forget that the improvement in the world economic situation for some means at the same time the marginalisation, if not the exclusion, of many others.

We all agree that there is no one global solution to the debt problem that will work for everyone. Cases are different and for the sake of the debate, let us identify the main different categories.

The poorest in the Third World, who are mostly in black Africa. A remarkable effort has been made to give some relief with regard to debt — mostly by the Europeans, insofar as most of the debt of black Africa is public debt. Measures which were proposed a long time ago were confirmed at the 1988 Toronto Summit, and are now well defined by the Paris Club, and they work.

---

*Member of the European Commission until 1 January 1989.

The Europeans have taken their full responsibility; at the same time they give direct assistance. They are not the only ones: the World Bank has a special programme for Africa; so has the United States. As far as the European Community is concerned, our action under the Lomé Convention means a substantial annual grant for development aid, and includes the Stabex system (under Stabex, stabilisation of export returns distributed some $280m in 1988). We intervene also through food aid programmes and emergency aid. Our formal grants to black Africa, or rather to the ACP countries of Africa, is of the order of $2.5 or $3bn per annum. In the Lomé IV negotiations the Community will insist that some of this money should be devoted to the support of adjustment policies, of a similar type to those recommended by the World Bank.

Let us turn to the rest of the Third World. First there are *the most advanced countries*, the four 'tigers' of East Asia and those that will soon be in a similar position. For them growing out of debt is no problem, and we should progressively integrate them into our ranks. It is essential that they should benefit from the liberalisation of trade, and that they should be treated like other industrial countries as soon as they have shown that they are competitive. In the Community we have started reducing the benefits of the General Scheme of Preferences for products where it is clearly demonstrated that they are competitive, one of the criteria being if in any one year an ldc has covered more than 20 per cent of the Community's imports of a single product.

Now we come to the main problem: *the heavily indebted middle-income countries*. May I first recall that the huge debt they have contracted was entered into in a different economic and financial environment. Rates of interest were not what they are now. It was a period when our banks were most anxious to recycle the large financial surpluses resulting from the oil crisis. It was also a period when our markets were demanding certain products, in particular raw materials and commodities, and this meant that part of their borrowing was then justified for such products, which are now in surplus.

Things have changed. Debt has accumulated to a total of say $1,000bn, 45 per cent of it in Latin America, and of this $350bn is owed to commercial banks. It is an unbearable burden, and debt service in Latin America represents something like 40-45 per cent of export returns. There have been years when the net transfer from Latin America to the industrialised countries — and even to the IMF — was of the order of $30bn. It is now reduced, but is still extremely heavy.

Nevertheless our own self-interest dictates that these economies should not be paralysed, that their growth should contribute to world growth. Herein lies a contradiction, already noted in the past, between the principle that having freely contracted, they must face up to their commitments and the fact that we should not impose on them an unbearable load of debt service and repayment.

References have been made to two similarly contradictory situations in the past, though they are completely different, and have a bearing on industrialised countries. First: Germany after World War I. The Allies had decided that there should be war reparations of $31bn but that the maximum to be paid annually should not exceed 25 per cent of export earnings. In fact, only $2bn were paid by the Weimar Republic, plus about $2bn funded by the Americans. Nevertheless we should remember the economic policies Germany had to undertake at that time and how they were universally seen as abusive, and finally what happened to the Weimar Republic. The second precedent occurred after World War II. Then, the approach was quite different. The United Kingdom owed the Americans some $20bn under lend lease. This was very much reduced to $650m. Then came the Marshall Plan; together with other transfers by the Americans $30bn were given to the West Europeans. Instead of pressing for the repayment of what was owed, the Americans agreed to lend us money. We have seen the results.

As I have said, the present debt situation is quite different. But we should not forget the contrast between the two approaches I have referred to. And we should note that in the present case a great effort has been made to see that debt repayments should be postponed and that debt service is lightened. With regard to public debt, this was done through the Paris Club — and between 1983 and 1987, 93 reschedulings were entered into for a total of $70bn. Of course it was more difficult with private creditors, with commercial banks. Advice was given; imaginative means of action were entered into: debt-equity swaps, debt reconversion, buy-backs. Two of the Western countries have suggested that we should go further and create a trust fund under the International Monetary Fund which would be in a position to guarantee bonds issued at a rebate against certain amounts of debt; this latter proposal has not yet been agreed. Still, there has been some alleviation of the burden of debt and debt service.

Let us now be clear: no real progress can occur without the right economic framework. Hence the demands by the International Monetary Fund, supported by the World Bank, at the request of all OECD countries, that the necessary macroeconomic policies should be entered into and followed. The World Bank's support of these adjustment policies has become extremely significant, and it is clear the European Community should and will support such an approach.

Nevertheless, I have one reservation about this. Economic discipline is certainly needed. But one should also recognise that there are political constraints, which are all the more serious in the case of countries which have gone in more deeply for state-run economies. It is far more difficult for Egypt to return to sound economic policies than it is for Tunisia; much more difficult for Argentina, after all the years of military rule, preceded by the years of the Peronista regime, than it is for others.

Therefore, political leaders of these countries should have a margin of flexibility in their timing. They should not be pressed unduly with regard to the calendar. May I tell you a story I heard recently in Cairo. I was told that a number of significant measures had been prepared, and even *decided* by the Head of State just before the events which happened in Algeria. The government — quite rightly in my opinion — was obliged to postpone the application of these measures. They will be implemented but then was not the proper time.

Up to now, in fact we have simply spoken of crisis management; there is a crisis, but how should it be managed? Obviously the priority is there, but not the whole answer. In fact, the amounts that have been rescheduled are limited, debt conversion as assessed by Mr Lawson amounts to a total of $25bn — a remarkable result, but very small in comparison with the size of the problem. What we have done is to help these countries to survive, not to develop.

So now let us try and take a longer-term perspective. These countries have a high demographic rate, and the rate of economic growth should at least match it, and match it for all. My first comment therefore, is that the return of growth and the profits of growth should be well shared. Our advice to them — maybe our conditionality — should bear not only on macroeconomic policies, but also on the political situation. It also implies more democracy. All the people should be associated with the decisions that are needed. Economic growth in Chile does not impress me, and I regret that Chile should so often be quoted as a model, particularly in Washington.

The dangers of injustice and corruption, particularly when this is widely publicised, are very great: they will jeopardise any beginnings of recovery. Look at what has happened in Algeria and how corruption and injustice were immediately denounced there. Look also at what has happened in Iran; under the Shah there was remarkable growth, but the people felt that there was no fair sharing.

All this being said, the main point, if we look at things from the longer perspective, is that these countries should have sufficient financial resources to finance development. First, then, let us try and help them cut their external payments:

— Debt and debt-service relief; the subject has already been addressed.
— Control of capital flight. This is an extremely difficult issue because capital flight is a direct result of poor policies and the proper answer would be development and growth.
— Reduction of imports is, of course, a priority. They should be helped to become self-sufficient, in particular in the field of agriculture and food production and, if not at the national level, at least at regional level. The European Community has entered into a systematic policy of support for what we call 'food strategy' which should result in self-sufficiency and wherever possible we try to implement it at the regional level. There are very few parts of the world where countries cannot achieve food self-sufficiency: Egypt perhaps, because of the shortage of arable land. In most of the Third World, it should be possible to achieve self-sufficiency, thanks to progress in agricultural technology — or should I say biogenetic revolution? It is good that the Community should be committed to supporting multi-annual programmes for a proper food strategy; and when I say food strategy it should have a bearing not only on production, but also on transport, storage, training and on pricing policies, without which there can be no successful food development.
— Of course one should also try to increase receipts, which means increasing exports.

The first condition which is stressed by everyone is that our markets should be opened. The present Uruguay Round plays an essential role in this respect. A proper functioning of the General System of Preferences is needed. The Community gives preferences to all ldcs, even those which do not vote as we would like them to in the United Nations.

Then we must also help them to produce what we are prepared to buy. This means adjusting their industries to the needs of the market. A prerequisite, however, is that we should be ready to accept with grace that they should promote new industries. We must accept a new division of labour. I am afraid I cannot say that public opinion is prepared for that at the moment. Personally, I think it is a shame that there is still a Multi-fibre Arrangement. It is highly regrettable that our governments should have refused to state formally that the present MFA is the last one. We must convince our governments and public opinion to accept a division of labour.

And we must help them to build modern industries, and modern services. For most of them, and in particular for the former colonies, the lack of technology is worse in services than in industry. This results from the simple fact that, in the colonial period, the indigenous labour forces were associated with production, while services were left entirely to the trading and transport companies of the metropolitan countries. No experience could be gained before independence. We should help now through training, transfer of technology, better information on what is required in our markets; most important are the services which will be instrumental in the development of external economic actions.

In my opinion the best approach in this respect is by encouraging joint-ventures. I think there is scope for a constantly growing number of joint-ventures, with a sharing of capital or simply with long-term contracts between partners. Encouragement, of course, means protection of investment, but it goes far beyond it.

Support for joint-ventures is all the more important since it mobilises small and medium-sized enterprises, which are most significant for a policy of development. I warmly approve the approach by the International Finance Corporation: during the 1987-8 financial year they have disbursed $760m for the support of such ventures as compared with $325m in 1985-6. The Community has only started in this field, e.g. through the provision of risk capital to be used by specialised financial agencies as part of larger risk-capital operations.

I consider the approach through joint-ventures to be also politically significant. Remember the old days after the first industrial revolution. It was then realised that industrialised countries needed raw materials and commodities which were to be found in what was not yet called the Third World. And this was one of the reasons for the colonial adventures. It was only after the independence of their colonies that the former colonial powers entered into co-operation over the supply of minerals and other raw materials, in order to safeguard their access to the mines and fields of production. If there now appears to be scope for more advanced industrial service development, it is important to turn immediately to a process of co-operation. And as private companies are the actors, this means joint-ventures rather than attempts to own these new industries and services. Part of the public aid available may well have to be allocated to the promotion of joint-ventures and the Community should confirm its policy in that regard.

All this being said, one fact remains: net inflows of capital are needed to supplement the resources of ldcs, to supplement their savings and earnings. This should normally be found in the international capital market; that is what James Baker highlighted in Seoul at the end of 1985. This did not work to the point where it is needed, so we should try and see what can be done.

First restore confidence, confidence of the commercial and financial markets in the creditworthiness of these countries. Guarantees should therefore be given, through association in joint-ventures, through the coverage of the first risks. Will this open up capital markets? I am not sure. Those with savings, the economies which have generated surplus, will naturally turn to the markets in deficit, but first to those that are in good shape; they will look for the most promising returns. And facing the supplies of capital, we find the gigantic appetite of the US financial market resulting from the present huge budget deficit. Naturally this will result also in high rates of interest in order to attract private sector savings.

The new financial instruments and the growth of mobile capital are well known. I am told that the present 'financial bubble' is of the order of $50,000 bn — against a total annual external trade in the world of $3,000 bn! There are days in New York when swaps between banks have reached $1,500bn, one half of the total value of trade in the world in one year. Can this go on unchecked indefinitely? Will not this accumulation of debt, American debt in particular, finally result in catastrophe?

What cannot be disputed is that all this means necessarily high rates of interest. And we know this is a major difficulty for fixed investments, more particularly for the debtor countries.

Coming to my conclusion, I realise I have said nothing new. You may, however, have noted that I have insisted on the globality of problems — global responsibility between us, the creditors, who are responsible, I dare say, as the main culprits for the present economic disorder. We, the three points of a triangle, Japan, North America and the Community, are the main actors in the field of trade; conditions of trade are decided in that triangle, so are monetary conditions and both apply to the rest of the world.

I also insist on globality because approaches to the problems must be comprehensive if any progress is to be made. There must be debt relief, but it will have no bearing if there is no chance for growth. Indebted countries must have sound economic policies, but growth will not take place if they are locked into a closed world on the margins of the industrialised world, in a ghetto of their own because they have no money and do not contribute to the growth. We also know that financing will not be available if there is not a return to more stability and predictability in our own markets. We cannot simply say that their problems are with us for a long time to come. The arithmetic of accumulated debt will make it more and more dangerous in the future and we all live together.

Marginalisation of the weak is not only morally unacceptable, it is economically and politically dangerous. More and more of them will doubt that our economic philosophy and structures are the right ones; the doubts will then shift to our political principles, and this will lead to totalitarianism. I am afraid of what is shaping up in Argentina. Violence is at the corner of every street. What young man would not despair when he has no chance for growth or an improvement of his situation, possibly no chance at all of a decent life? And this despair will lead to violence, which may give the opportunity for an abusive domination by pretended spiritual forces, and lead to fundamentalism. In a large part of the world, the most advanced part of the Third World, the part that has the longest history behind it, we are ourselves building up the forces that will result in totalitarianism and fundamentalism.

The European Community has its responsibility and has its full part to play, particularly in using its influence on the other two points of the triangle, and especially on the United States, in order that liberty and democracy should be protected and promoted and that growth should extend to all and not only to the rich and powerful. This means — and I am not embarrassed to say this — that public authorities must take their responsibility; they cannot leave it to market forces to rule the world. Of course, it is the market that provides the parameters of development, it is market forces that should be responsible for production and distribution. But public authorities, elected Parliaments, governments, the European Commission have a duty to all the people in the world, and not only to those that produce the present growth and benefit from it.

13:
Some Other Issues

Lord Lever of Manchester

> The . . . duty of the sovereign or commonwealth is that of
> erecting and maintaining those public institutions and those
> public works, which, though they may be in the highest
> degree advantageous to a great society, are, however, of such
> a nature that the profit could never repay the expense to any
> individual or small number of individuals, and which it
> therefore cannot be expected that any individual or small
> number of individuals should erect or maintain.
>
> Adam Smith, *The Wealth of Nations*, Book V pp210-211

We all too rarely hear these words of Adam Smith from *The Wealth
of Nations*. There are no free lunches even in the international field.
The little homily of Adam Smith is repudiated by both left-wingers
and right-wingers, but all over the world institutions are erected
which run at a loss but collectively give us the greatest and most
necessary advantages, such as the health service and so on.

In the early part of this century, our block-headed leaders
neglected their duty to create such institutions to serve the
increasingly globalised economy. In 1945 the rudiments were
established of those international institutions which were required
to make this interdependent economy workable — the IMF, the
World Bank and the GATT. As a result we have had a remarkable
advance in 40 years, a wealth of creation and globalisation and
interdependence, but far from advancing these institutions, we
have if anything regressed in that area. Emphasis is now needed
to advance the collective institutions which will bear the risks and
losses to some extent, in partnership no doubt with the private
banking system required to fulfil these crucial responsibilities.

Stephany Griffith-Jones, Institute of Development Studies, University of Sussex

Certain elements of costs of the debt crisis, particularly in the Third
World, have been powerfully brought out in earlier papers, and

Richard Jolly outlined the human costs of adjustment. It is not just that development has been stopped or even retarded in the Third World. The hope of development of a better future has been lost. And that in psychological terms is a greater loss than some of the human tragedies we have seen. We need the renewal of hope for the future, to which a more satisfactory way forward on the debt problem could make a major contribution.

Another cost is the cost to the developed countries in terms of trade lost with the developing world. It is estimated that at least six million jobs have been lost in the European Community, 300,000 of them in the UK. So that if an alternative solution were found to the debt problem, much greater employment, much greater economic activity and much greater trade would result between creditor and debtor nations. This is not just a question of looking at the balance between debtors and creditors but between different groups within the creditor nations.

It is unlikely that there will be any significant private lending to developing countries in the next 10 or 15 years. From a development point of view, this is in itself in the long term not a bad thing because variable-interest, relatively short-term lending is not the most appropriate mechanism to fund development. One of the main assumptions of previous debt crisis management strategy, which was to restore creditworthiness, is not therefore really going to work. There should therefore be some kind of coalition formed between those who believe in development, for whatever reasons, and those who believe in the market, and we should look for a market solution. Up to now governments have mainly been encouraging new lending from private banks because they saw that as the key objective, namely, to preserve the stability of the international banking system. For this objective you need to keep servicing the debt at 100 per cent, and the problem, which involves only a few large US and British banks, can be handled by a case-by-case approach. The main challenge now, however, to the international community is not the fragility of the banking system, but the stagnation in major parts of the Third World. The new debt strategy should therefore address this issue by focusing the attention of governments, through the mechanisms that John Williamson and others have outlined, on reducing the value of the debt by making greater use of the market mechanism and stressing less the issue of new lending.

A final point is the scale of the problem. If one takes account of the fact that banks have already provisioned to an important extent against part of the possible loss, and that an additional income would be generated to Britain through trade flows through the greater employment resulting, then the cost of such a solution over a 10-year period might be not much more than £2 per year per taxpayer. It is important to reduce this to a personal level and to give a clear dimension of what a major boost to development on the one side could imply, what the maximum cost to creditors and taxpayers might be, and also what the potential benefits to traders and investors in those parts of the developing world could be.

Euan Macdonald, S.G. Warburg and Co.

As has often been the case in economic history, the system which has developed for dealing with the debt crisis is entirely haphazard. The whole Paris Club rescheduling process has worked in one sense extremely well, and in another sense rather badly. It takes up an enormous amount of time and it postpones all the problems from one year to the next. What some private banks are now trying to do is to reverse the whole process. Instead of having an IMF analysis, which tries to determine what the financing gap of each country is every time it gets itself into trouble by adding up all the outflows and all the inflows, and then trying to find a way of filling that gap by rescheduling, they are trying to get the IMF and other interested bodies to take a view on what the essential inflows and outflows are and then to look at debt service as a residual. That is to say, instead of saying that Nigeria is $5bn short this year, to do the sums and say Nigeria could afford $1bn debt service. Whatever is available can then be distributed equably amongst the creditors. At the same time, some part of the payment, even if it is quite small, must be allocated to the reduction of principal outstanding, because otherwise the principal continues to grow and the problem is never solved.

What was agreed at the Toronto summit of 1988 comes slightly closer to this kind of analysis. But it is also the case that in the two examples so far when the Toronto terms were applied — in Mali and in Madagascar — it was quite clear that neither country would actually be able to afford what was agreed because the concessionality was insufficient.

The first thing that needs to be done to achieve progress is to persuade the new US Administration that giving 25 or 18 years grace or whatever at the market rates of interest is not concessionality at all, and that even if it was spread over 100 years on those terms it would not help. If the Americans can be persuaded to go along with the genuine Toronto terms and those terms can be made even more generous, then something could be done.

With the problem of debt service out of the way by this method, a much more interesting and fruitful exercise could be embarked upon. It is not difficult to persuade banks to lend to the Third World particularly on trade finance which is a great deal more profitable in medium-term lending in any case. And as soon as there is the slightest chance that even a substantial debtor country can service new trade finance lines, those lines are not at all difficult to organise.

The Rt Hon. David Howell MP, Chairman, House of Commons Select Committee on Foreign Affairs

The approach so far seems to imply that there is a great choice between the adjustment process and outright support programmes to reach the poorest sectors of Third World societies. This is not so. There is not only room for both but both approaches are absolutely vital.

Secondly, there is an important contrast between helping the poorest and the most vulnerable inside any society or nation, which is a very intimate and local affair, and the development process which is a very highly internationalised business. One cannot just ring-fence a particular economy and say within this let there be development. That experiment has been tried and has failed in the centrally planned regimes, which are now trying to re-join the international trading system because that is the only way to secure development within society. As to the nature of the structure of the international system that we need, again it is not a choice between government's collective and private enterprise action; both have to go together in combination. We are seeing a powerful new player enter the stage. The Japanese are going to be, if not already the largest aid donors, certainly the decisive actors in the world system and we must factor their actions and their attitudes into the policy mix.

Aid through grants, rather than loans, from official sources remains an essential ingredient of the package. Debt reduction is making a little progress. There does need to be, and well structured debt equity schemes can offer this, a more positive opening and a more positive prospect. We must recognise first of all that the character of world investment has changed, and secondly that the character of the multinational structure has changed. Today's Asian and particularly the Japanese multinationals are talking a different language. They have learned some of the lessons that the Americans painfully learned in the 1960s.

The third part of the international package is reduced protection which could by itself vastly increase the potential of the developing countries. The fourth part is that the developing countries should maintain steady growth and low interest rates.

Fifthly we cannot assume that there is ever going to be in the pattern of future development a further massive support generally for commodity prices. We are simply moving out of the energy-intensive raw material-intensive age. The main content of all the products traded now is knowledge, education and skill, not raw materials, and where it is raw materials, there are innovators trying to design out the need for oil, for metals, even for foodstuff supplies. Therefore wise economies now recognise that they have got to put the full emphasis on processing, on value added and indeed on high technology and skills. Those are the raw materials of the future and therefore what any development aid, public or private, has to concentrate on is enabling the less developed and developing world to raise its skills and its knowledge intensity.

Nicholas Wolfers, Midland Bank

It is important to remember that during the period of the oil crisis of the 1970s, far from the banks telling the government to get off their backs, they were actually responding in good part in their recycling efforts to the massive imbalance in the world financial system. To some extent the problem was that they acted quickly and in a way that everyone at the time deemed appropriate, but with one major disadvantage, namely that in no sense did they have anything like the sovereign standing that governments or international financial institutions had, to deal with other governments. They therefore discovered that money spent for well-designed projects, let alone general purpose funding, did not always end up as they expected and there was nothing they could do about it. The correct role for the banks at the present stage is to move into the area of trade finance, an area that they know well.

In a period of falling commercial interest rates round the world we saw a good deal less interest from borrowers of all kinds to use official export credit because it takes longer to organise than commercial credit. But at a time when interest rates still seem to be on the rise around the world, the attractions of fixed-rate, medium- and long-term financings supported by government guarantees are much greater. Exceptions can now be made by national credit agencies in a positive way to get free-standing viable projects off the ground more quickly and this in obvious senses can be more than a little valuable to the export-generating and the foreign exchange-earning capacity of the debtor countries.

The role of banks should be seen not only as lenders but also as catalysts for change in a variety of ways. The investment banks have been extremely active in this field. There is also a role for the banks in the important job of strengthening the management of individual corporations in a variety of countries in institution building. The banks also have a major role in training, as there has been increasing recognition of the importance of tight financial management in all parts of the world.

Finally the use and direction of Japanese aid which was originally very much geared to its own geographical region, but is now moving to Africa and Latin America, is a major issue for the banks, and also a major message of hope. In the Asian region, the aims of establishing inter-regional trade and co-operation have really begun to take off and bear fruit.

Professor Mike Faber, Institute of Development Studies, University of Sussex

The impossibility of reaching a situation of agreement in advance on a solution of the debt problem does not necessarily preclude the possibility of reaching acceptance in retrospect as the result of a new situation created by a unilateral action by one of the main debtor nations. Many of the schemes of debt reduction, if they are going to be accomplished on a major scale, if the commercial banks are going to play, if we are going to have the kind of buy-back schemes, the competitive debt tendering, the securitisation of lower interest rates and some of the schemes which the World Bank would love to get involved with, if only the American government and a few others would encourage them to do so, will only take place when that new situation has been created. The most interesting area of territory so far unexposed in these papers is what the design of the unilateral action by that debtor should be, and what the reaction of the international financial institutions and the OECD governments should be when that action has been taken. But to explore debt default would require another book . . .

Also available

ALL PARTY PARLIAMENTARY GROUP ON OVERSEAS DEVELOPMENT

Managing Third World Debt

The Third World's debt burden has become a barrier to development, for low income countries as well as for Latin America. Overall, Third World countries are now exporting capital back to us. This, the second report of the All Party Parliamentary Group recognises that economic growth must be part of the solution, rather than the pay-off after years of austerity.

Debt Working Party of the All Party Parliamentary Group on Overseas Development.
Chairman, Bowen Wells MP.

"An excellent brief study". **The Guardian**

"For the . . . reader who wants a quick introduction to the subject this . . . admirably fits the bill". Graham Bird,
Third World Quarterly

76 pages, 1987, £3.95, ISBN 0 85003 107 9

UK Aid to African Agriculture

This, the first report of the All Party Parliamentary Group on Overseas Development, concludes that the successes of the UK aid programme in support of agricultural development in Africa outweigh its weaknesses and disappointments but there is an urgent need for more official aid in the sector.

Working Party of the All Party Parliamentary Group on Overseas Development.
Chairman, Jim Lester MP.

64 pages, 1985, £2.95, ISBN 0 85003 099 4